Also by Jimmie L. Hancock

All the Questions in the Bible

~

New Millennium Calendar
(Study the Bible Daily in the Year 2000)

~

A New View of Proverbs

~

Revelation: The Fifth Gospel

~

A Devotional Commentary on John's Gospel

~

Bad News from the Good Book

~

Forever Prayer

IN FEAR OF
GOD

Jimmie L. Hancock

WESTBOW
PRESS®
A DIVISION OF THOMAS NELSON
& ZONDERVAN

WestBow Press books may be ordered through booksellers or by contacting:

WestBow Press
A Division of Thomas Nelson & Zondervan
1663 Liberty Drive
Bloomington, IN 47403
www.westbowpress.com
1 (866) 928-1240

Scripture quotations taken from The Holy Bible, New International Version® NIV® Copyright © 1973 1978 1984 2011 by Biblica, Inc. TM. Used by permission. All rights reserved worldwide.

Scripture taken from the King James Version of the Bible.

Scripture taken from the Contemporary English Version © 1991, 1992, 1995 by American Bible Society. Used by Permission

ISBN: 978-1-9736-8946-1 (sc)
ISBN: 978-1-9736-8945-4 (e)

Print information available on the last page.

WestBow Press rev. date: 4/8/2020

DEDICATION TO MY FATHER

My father, James William Hancock, was born March 10, 1883 in Belton, South Carolina. After the death of his first wife Maggie Lollis in 1919, he married my mother Samatha Caroline Bannister on December 25, 1932. My father was 54 and my mother 37 when I was born on November 18, 1937. My father died March 5, 1957. My mother died on July 5, 1989. I was the only child my parents had together. I inherited 11 half-brothers and sisters, 8 on Dad's side and 3 on Mom's side. I remember a few things about my father which are fond memories for me, like when he took me fishing; when he bought me my first drum so I could play in the school band; when he built me a race cart so I could participate with my friends in the downhill road races in front of our house; when I met him coming home from his cotton mill job and he gave me a leftover jelly biscuit from his lunch Mom had made for him; when he brought me my lunch to school one day when I forgot it; when I watched him defrosting water pipes under our house during a cold winter; when he deliberately drove over the bumps in the road when we went riding in his A-Model Ford; when he bought me a toy "tin" water pump to play with; when he took me to see the trains go by in Belton; when he bought me a "box" of peanuts and I found a nickel inside; when he took the time to teach me how to count to 29 in a funny fast way by speaking in a kind of limerick fashion; and...well, he was my father, bigger than I, older than I, smarter than I and I loved him. If I feared him, it was because he had lived in worlds I knew nothing about. But I was never afraid of him. I dedicated a previous book to my Mother. I dedicate this book in memory of my Father.

My Father and Mother, 1932

A GUIDE TO CONTENTS

GETTING STARTED

It was 1949 and I was twelve years of age when William Adger Grey asked me to serve as a ticket-taker at the Joy Theatre which he owned in my home town of Belton, South Carolina. It was my first job and I was paid free admission to watch the movies! I can't remember when I didn't like watching movies, especially "Westerns" made in the 1930s, 40s, and 50s. Remember the song by the Statler Brothers entitled "Whatever Happened to Randolph Scott"? Well, he's still around. I own collections of movies starring Randolph Scott, Lash LaRue, Tex Ritter, Gene Autry, Roy Rogers, the Durango Kid, Johnny "Mack" Brown, Allen "Rocky" Lane, Tim Holt, Smiley Burnette, and many others. I recently watched a movie on Turner Classic Movies entitled "The Durango Kid" made in 1940 which starred Charles Starrett in his first episode of the Durango Kid series of films. It was released by Columbia Pictures Corporation in black and white and was one hour long. Something interesting happened, at least to me, while watching the film. It was about half-way through at a point when Charles Starrett was talking with Kenneth MacDonald, the bad guy. MacDonald became irritated during the conversation because of something Starrett was explaining to him, and MacDonald said to Starrett, "Never mind all that palaver. What about the Durango Kid? Is he here?" The interesting thing about it was that I didn't know what "palaver" meant despite my years of formal education.

I had to pause the movie which I had recorded and re-run the conversation again. Now what was that word being used in a western movie in 1940? So, I looked it up. It's been around since the mid-18th century when trading took place between African natives and European explorers as each side tried to persuade the other to get the best deal in the trade. The word derived from the Portuguese palavra meaning word and from the Latin parabola meaning comparison. It later came to mean, among other things, talking for a long time without getting anywhere. In other words, MacDonald was telling Starrett to cut the nonsense (palaver) and get down to business![1]

Useless talk. There's much in the Bible about useless talk. For instance, talking about things that have little or no value. In the Book of Job, Eliphaz falsely accuses Job (in my opinion), but speaks wisely (in my opinion) when he asks: *Would a wise person answer with empty notions or fill their belly with the hot east wind? Would they argue with useless words, with speeches that have no value?*[2] Consider what the Apostle Paul wrote to Timothy: *Keep reminding God's people of these things. Warn them before God against quarreling about words; it is of no value, and only ruins those who listen.*[3] Paul also wrote to Titus: *But avoid foolish controversies and genealogies and arguments and quarrels about the law, because these are unprofitable and useless.*[4] And keep in mind what Jesus said about speaking careless words: *But I tell you that everyone will have to give account on the day of judgment for every empty word they have*

---

[1] Another Western movie that uses the word "palaver" is the 1964 "The Outrage" starring Paul Newman, Lawrence Harvey, Claire Bloom, Edward G. Robinson, and William Shatner. Shatner plays a minister to whom Robinson makes mention of his "holy palaver".

[2] Job 15:2-3 (All Scripture is in italics with no verse numbers)

[3] 2 Timothy 2:14

[4] Titus 3:9

spoken. For by your words you will be acquitted, and by your words you will be condemned.[5]

I want to make clear that if we desire to maintain a proper relationship with God, we need to make sure we are doing what God requires us to do or not do. Among other things, make sure any palavering we do results in less useless talk and more in our being faithful followers of Jesus of whom God said: *This is my Son, whom I love; with him I am well pleased.*[6] When Jesus was twelve years old, he was found by his parents Joseph and Mary in the temple courts in Jerusalem. Jesus was doing a little palavering himself, but he wasn't talking nonsense! He was: *...sitting among the teachers, listening to them and asking them questions. Everyone who heard him was amazed at his understanding and his answers.*[7] When his parents expressed that they had been *...anxiously searching for you,* Jesus replied: *Didn't you know I had to be in my Father's house.*[8] In other words, why were you searching for me? You should have known where I would be. The King James Version has: *...wist ye not that I must be about my Father's business?* In the Greek New Testament, there is no word following "Father's". That is, it literally could be translated (NIV): "Didn't you know I had to be in my Father's?" and (KJV): "...wist ye not that I must be about my Father's?" Jesus was where he should have been expected to be, in his Father's house and about his Father's business! We too should: *Always be prepared to give an answer to everyone who asks you to give the reason for the hope that you have.*[9]

We Christians are in the business of relating to our Heavenly Father, to His Holy Spirit and to His Son Jesus the Christ—the

---

[5] Matthew 12:36-37
[6] Matthew 3:17
[7] Luke 2:46-47
[8] Luke 2:48-49
[9] 1 Peter 3:15

Messiah, the Anointed One. I like that word "relating". It implies closeness, faithfulness and love. Relating also implies family—relatives. Families are supposed to look after one another producing "close family ties". When we say "the family of God" we are talking about being "brothers and sisters" under the authority of God through His Son Jesus who is our Lord and Savior, and with guidance by the power of the Holy Spirit. And the theme of "love" is paramount in the Bible as the central working relational power that binds and holds the family together: *...love one another.*[10] Now, what I want to do in this book is introduce another theme into this family picture—a theme that is also necessary for the spiritual family binding process. You may disagree with what I have to say and want to close this book immediately. I'm hoping you will not do that but consider seriously what I have to say. It is Biblically sound. It just isn't emphasized much and we all suffer in our spiritual growth when we neglect it. Actually, it is just recently since I have encountered this aspect of "relating" to God. The relational theme I want to emphasize seems so unnatural; yet, without it, any relative fullness of knowing God is never within reach. This necessary theme is "Fearing God": *The fear of the LORD is the beginning of wisdom; all who follow his precepts have good understanding. To him belongs eternal praise.*[11] In typical Hebrew parallelism, fear of God and following his precepts and praising God are definitely related.

Others have made mention of Bible references about fearing God and also to references about how we should not be dominated by fear. So what's the difference with what I'm proposing? What I generally read and hear about fear is that the Bible has a lot to say about how God does not want us to live in fear. And when it comes to verses about fearing God, the comments are generally

---

[10] John 13:34
[11] Psalm 111:10

about having reverence for God. And while it is proper to have reverence for God, reverence and fear should be seen together and work together when it comes to our relating to God. The Bible says we are to fear God. And such fear includes following after what God wants us to do. We should fear God, knowing that when we disobey him we are subject to his displeasure and possible discipline. Indeed, there are references in the Bible in which God communicates with those faithful to him that they should not be afraid: *After this, the word of the LORD came to Abram in a vision: Do not be afraid, Abram. I am your shield, your very great reward.*[12] King David spoke to his son Solomon: *May the LORD give you discretion and understanding when he puts you in command over Israel, so that you may keep the law of the LORD your God. Then you will have success if you are careful to observe the decrees and laws that the LORD gave Moses for Israel. Be strong and courageous. Do not be afraid or discouraged.*[13] It appears to me that this concept of being told not to be afraid implies that when we are faithful to God we should have no fear of the problems we might face in life and even no fear of God. But having no fear of God is wrong. I hope to show that the Bible has references in which it is expected that having fear toward God is acceptable and even demanded. One such reference in which both ideas are mentioned is when Moses said to the Israelites: *Do not be afraid. God has come to test you, so that the fear of God will be with you to keep you from sinning.*[14] The latter part of this verse about the fear of God does not mean fear that belongs to God. It means fear toward God. That's the idea I want to explore. And also, how does fear toward God keep me from sinning?

When the Psalmist asked: *The LORD is my light and my*

---

[12] Genesis 15:1

[13] 1 Chronicles 22:12-13

[14] Exodus 20:20

salvation — whom shall I fear? The LORD is the stronghold of my life — of whom shall I be afraid?[15] there is no hint of being afraid of God Himself. But when the Pharaoh of Egypt was asking Moses for prayer to God to stop the thunder and hail, Moses said: *But I know that you and your officials still do not fear the LORD God?*[16] Such fear directly applies to God. Moses told the Israelites: *These are the commands, decrees and laws the LORD your God directed me to teach you to observe in the land that you are crossing the Jordan to possess, so that you, your children and their children after them may fear the LORD your God as long as you live by keeping all his decrees and commands that I give you, and so that you may enjoy long life.*[17] Moses also said to the Israelites: *Fear the LORD your God, serve him only and take your oaths in his name.*[18] He also added that they were not to follow other gods because the Lord God was a jealous God and would destroy them. They were to obey God's commands and do what was right and good in His sight.[19] Moses concluded that: *...if we are careful to obey all this law before the LORD our God, as he has commanded us, that will be our righteousness.*[20] Fearing God is not to be afraid of God and run away from him, but to know his majestic power and live in close harmony with him. Fear toward God is therefore part of anyone's relationship with God, whether you follow him or not. The Christian perspective includes fear toward God. The One and Only God who is a Loving Father came to us as his Only Son and shared life with us and gave his life for us. He took our place as the wages of sin. Not as sin but as the wages of sin—death. And he overcame death to become our Lord and Savior and Redeemer. How can we not submit to him whose

---

[15] Psalms 27:1

[16] Exodus 9:30

[17] Deuteronomy 6:1-2

[18] Deuteronomy 6:13

[19] See Deuteronomy 6:14-19

[20] Deuteronomy 6:25

Spirit is our seal of everlasting life? How can we be filled with his loving Spirit and not be gripped with fear of his majesty—fear that captivates us and compels us to follow his righteousness? Not fear that repels us but fear that indwells us and draws us closer always to his commandments and to his yearning for our good and safety—fear that forms a bond of intimacy. People with just love are spoiled disciples—they are easily driven to isolation and selfishness. Love without fear is dangerous. Fear brings us closer to the core of God's very nature.

People who see God with fear in their hearts are those who see what Job saw when he finally met God: *My ears had heard of you but now my eyes have seen you. Therefore I despise myself and repent in dust and ashes.*[21]

~

They hear what Paul heard when he ventured to paradise: *...and heard inexpressible things, things that no one is permitted to tell.*[22]

~

They respond the way Moses felt at the burning bush: *At this, Moses hid his face, because he was afraid to look at God.*[23]

~

They hear what Peter endured when he refused to listen and believe Jesus: *Jesus turned and said to Peter, Get behind me, Satan!*

---

[21] Job 42:5-6
[22] 2 Corinthians 12:3-4
[23] Exodus 3:5-6 (See also the account in Acts 7:32 which adds that Moses trembled with fear.)

You are a stumbling block to me; you do not have in mind the concerns of God, but merely human concerns.[24]

~

They understand the hardship of Adam when God banished him from the Garden of Eden: *Cursed is the ground because of you; through painful toil you will eat food from it all the days of your life.... until you return to the ground, since from it you were taken; for dust you are and to dust you will return.*[25]

~

They know the glory of the doubting Thomas who, seeing the Risen Jesus, said: *My Lord and my God!*[26]

~

They identify with the faith shown by the Roman Centurion who said to Jesus: *Lord, I do not deserve to have you come under my roof. But just say the word, and my servant will be healed.*[27]

~

People with fear toward God as well as love understand John the Baptist who saw Jesus and said: *Look, the Lamb of God, who takes away the sin of the world!*[28] And who later said: *He must become greater; I must become less.*[29]

---

[24] Matthew 16:23
[25] Genesis 3:17-19
[26] John 20:28
[27] Matthew 8:8
[28] John 1:29
[29] John 3:30

They understand the hardship of Christian living as well as its blessings and spiritual powers. They understand the freedom and the servitude of dedication to Jesus. Being a Christian is a call to commitment, hardship, and danger. When God puts his hand upon us, it's not just to grant us peace and happiness but also purpose and guidance, love and devotion, and accountability. So, in addition to our call to love God, we are called to fear him—and also to glorify him. The Psalmist points us toward this latter goal: *Teach me your way, LORD, that I may rely on your faithfulness; give me an undivided heart, that I may fear your name. I will praise you, Lord my God, with all my heart; I will glorify your name forever. For great is your love toward me; you have delivered me from the depths, from the realm of the dead.*[30] C. S. Lewis reminds us that "In commanding us to glorify Him, God is inviting us to enjoy Him."[31] In the midst of love and fear, there is glory and joy. To enjoy God is to experience God's peace, which transcends all understanding.[32]

I was once a magician. I was a teenager back in mid-1950 when a professional magician came to town and put on a show at our recreational center in Anderson, South Carolina. He arrived in town a week before the show and left a wooden box open for inspection for several days in the lobby of our downtown bank. On the night of the show, the box trick was the final performance of the evening. The mayor and other dignitaries came on stage and nailed the box shut with the magician inside. It was a smash success when the magician escaped, and I was hooked on doing magic tricks. I read everything available in our area about magic tricks and even as an adult continued to entertain small groups

---

[30] Psalms 86:11-13

[31] C. S. Lewis, *The Joyful Christian*, (New York: Macmillan Publishing Co., Inc., 1977), p. 120.

[32] See Philippians 4:4-9

with enthusiasm and enjoyment and participated in putting on free shows for the community. I was a 25-year member of the Society of American Magicians and also belonged to the International Brotherhood of Magicians. I taught a class in magic at a local community college. I was a good magician and still possess a fine library of magic books. But I was not a professional. It was just a hobby. The reason I know I was never a magician of any real worth is simple—I met a few who were, and they were in a group whose talent I could never attain. And that's the way it is with a lot of people who are enthusiastic about their Christian faith and religious life. They are people who enjoy what they believe in and the life they have chosen to live. They really are good people. It's even more than a hobby. They practice what they believe in. They're not hypocrites. They're just not perfect even when they try to be! They're in love with Jesus and they know that every day they live is an opportunity to express their devotion to God. Whether they know it or not, that love is coupled with a special kind of fear—a fear that they can never attain to all of God's expectations. If this fear is understood and used properly it's possible to be very successful as a Christian disciple, realizing we may even show hospitality to angels.[33]

---

[33] Hebrews 12:28—13:3 (The KJV uses the term fear)

DISCOVERING FEAR TOWARD GOD

Now all has been heard;
here is the conclusion of the matter:
Fear God and keep his commandments,
for this is the duty of all mankind.
For God will bring every deed into judgment,
including every hidden thing,
whether it is good or evil.[34]

I found it interesting that the Holman Bible Dictionary[35] gave a lengthy explanation of "Fear" whereas The Illustrated Dictionary & Concordance of the Bible[36] had no reference to the topic. As mentioned earlier, reverence is a major concern when defining fear toward God. The Holman Bible Dictionary is no exception: "God's work, His power, majesty, and holiness evoke fear and demand acknowledgment. The fear of God is not to be understood as the dread that comes out of fear of punishment, but as the reverential regard and the awe that comes out of recognition and submission to the divine. It is the revelation of God's will to which

---

[34] Ecclesiastes 12:13-14

[35] Trent C. Butler, Ph.D., General Editor, *Holman Bible Dictionary* (Nashville: Holman Bible Publishers, 1991), pp. 480-482.

[36] Geoffrey Wigoder, Ph.D., General Editor, *The Illustrated Dictionary & Concordance of the Bible* (New York: Sterling Publishing, 2005).

the believer submits in obedience."[37] No Biblical references were given for this opinion. Again, while reverence and awe must be taken into account, fear towards God's majesty is more than just reverence and awe. As we shall discover, it also involves discipline. Inherent in any fear is the absence of personal control. To fear God is to know that God is in total control. Looking back at the Biblical story of Moses' encounter with God at the Burning Bush,[38] I noticed that Moses replied to God's call with the words: *Here I am*. Then God said to Moses: *I am sending you to Pharaoh to bring my people the Israelites out of Egypt*. Then Moses replied: *Who am I, that I should go to Pharaoh and bring the Israelites out of Egypt?* God's reply to Moses was: *I AM WHO I AM*. *This is what you are to say to the Israelites: I AM has sent me to you*. This is total control by God who demands fear. I like the story about the three umpires discussing their craft. One said "I call them as I see them." The next one said: "I call them as they are." The third one said, "They are as I call them!" If you were suited up, put in a rocket ship and sent into outer space, then ejected and found yourself floating about on your own with no help in sight, I'm sure you would be filled with awe and reverence. I'm also quite sure you would be afraid.

Let me tell you about an experience I had on June 28, 2018, while driving to my Edgewater, Florida home. It took place at a Rest Area on I-75 just South of Tifton, Georgia. While parked at the Rest Area, I was sitting in my 2016 Ford Focus with the motor running. I was the only person in the car. The time was mid-morning, approximately 10:30 a.m. It was a very warm day, the air-conditioner was on, and I was eating a banana. I thought the car was in park and did not think I was doing anything wrong. I noticed a waste can on the sidewalk just outside my car. My

---

[37] *Holman Bible Dictionary*, p.481.
[38] See Exodus 3:1-15 (My underlining for emphasis)

intention was to step outside and get rid of my banana peeling. Just as I was opening the door to exit, I felt the car moving. Within just a second or two, I was thrown from the vehicle and when I lifted my head to see what had happened, I was lying partially under the car and watched the left front tire run over my left ankle and my right thigh. The car continued to move slowly backwards across the roadway. I got up and caught up with the vehicle, was able to get in the car as it was moving and I was able to stop the car before it hit anything. As weird as it sounds, that's exactly what happened as I experienced it. After I stopped the car, I sat in the car and called 911 on my cell phone. The emergency vehicle responders must have notified the highway patrol because an officer arrived shortly afterwards. I told him what had happened. He was extremely nice but I'm not sure he believed me! He did not write a citation and after the emergency ambulance arrived, the officer saw to it that my car was safely parked, locked and I was given the keys. He also said someone would come by and check on my car over the next few days. I was transported to the Tift Regional Medical Center in Tifton, Georgia. I was in no severe pain. I was given a series of X-rays and admitted overnight for observation. I was told that no bones were broken. My right thigh developed a hematoma which stayed around for the next several months, but I was able to walk the next day. I was released from the hospital the afternoon of the next day, having spent one night at the hospital. I had no friends in that area, my daughter lives in Atlanta, Georgia, and my son lives in Fairborn, Ohio. My wife had died of brain cancer just two months earlier. I was alone and without any help to get to my car which was still at the Rest Area. I wanted to get to a local motel and stay there for a couple of days, then try to drive on to my home in Florida. Fortunately, a hospital nurse put me in touch with a group from the First Baptist Church in Tifton, Georgia, which helped people involved in accidents in their area along I-75.

After I was released from the hospital, a Church volunteer named Wilbur Webb came out and picked me up at the hospital and took me to a nearby Motel. Wilbur then assisted me in getting my car to the Motel. He also helped me return in a couple of days to the Hospital Emergency Room for a checkup. I was told again that my condition was good and that I could drive on to Florida. I had no further complications, and I am now completely healed.

Now let me tell you what I learned from my experience. First, I learned not to sit in my car with the motor idling without the door being locked, and my seatbelt and hand break engaged! Second, I learned to fear God. I learned that God is really the one who is in charge of my life. Yes, I'm often awed by God. Yes, I try to always maintain reverence toward God. And yes, I fear God. I love him and I fear him. There was a time when I knew what was right and what was wrong—and did what was wrong in spite of what I knew was wrong. And sometimes I still do! But I now have better control over what I choose to do. When I fail to do what I know I should do, I know God's grace is there to help me. But my fear of God helps me to be a better person by making better choices in life. I wish I had known about fearing God in this manner at an earlier age. If I had, I'm quite sure I would not have made as many mistakes as I have made in life. I'm not saying I wish something like my accident could have occurred earlier in my life. I just wish I had been taught more about fearing God as well as about loving God. My communication with God is not perfect, but I am trying to better understand his language. It's a lot like trying to learn Hebrew—reading from right to left, reading words that aren't separated, have no vowels, no punctuation, and no capital letters. Yet, being friends with God, a phrase my wife often used, is based on my wanting to know him better and to develop a listening ear that goes even further than just reading the Bible. It's hard but when it happens, it's very joyful! I really try hard each day to get it right and lessen the fear of failure, not the fear of God. God is never wrong. And when I know what is wrong, I know I will be better off to avoid it, which opens the door to better understanding the relationship God and I have together.

Bad things happen all the time. The Bible is often called The Good Book. Actually, the Bible is filled with many bad things occurring that don't make for appropriate bed-time stories. For instance, in the very first book of the Bible—the Book of Genesis—in the Garden of Eden, we find a snake leading Adam and Eve astray! And soon after that, Cain kills his brother Abel! In fact, I found so many bad things that I listed them all in a book entitled "Bad Things from the Good Book". I found that God was responsible for many of the unfortunate happenings in the Bible. Take for example when God brought on the flood: *The LORD saw how great the wickedness of the human race had become on the earth, and that every inclination of the thoughts of the human heart was only evil all the time. The LORD regretted that he had made human beings on the earth, and his heart was deeply troubled. So the LORD said, I will wipe from the face of the earth the human race I have created — and with them the animals, the birds and the creatures that move along the ground — for I regret that I have made them. But Noah found favor in the eyes of the LORD.*[39]

Reflecting on all those bad things in the Bible, especially the ones directly caused by God, is very disturbing. From an early age, I've always enjoyed reading and studying the Bible. I've learned that I don't have to understand everything in the Bible in order to appreciate its value to my life. There are a couple of major things I don't understand in the Bible. I have read the explanations given by reputable Biblical scholars, but still don't have a satisfactory

---

[39] Genesis 6:5-8

answer for myself. I'm not saying these events are untrue. I just don't understand them.

The first incident is found in Genesis, Chapter 22. God tested Abraham, telling him to sacrifice his only son Isaac as a burnt offering. Abraham made all the necessary preparations and, according to the record: *...he reached out his hand and took the knife to slay his son.*[40] The picture I've always had of this moment is commonly illustrated showing Abraham holding the knife above his bound son and is obviously about to come down with the knife and kill his son. I really don't know if this is what happened or not. The record only says that Abraham reached for the knife. I can only imagine what must have been going on in the mind of Abraham. Would he really be capable of doing this? As the story goes, Abraham was interrupted by an angel of God who told him not to harm Isaac: *Do not lay a hand on the boy, he said. Do not do anything to him. Now I know that you fear God, because you have not withheld from me your son, your only son.*[41] Then Abraham saw a ram caught in a thicket and sacrificed the ram as a burnt offering in place of his son Isaac. From a Christian perspective, I know how this story relates to the death of Jesus on the Cross of Calvary when God did not provide a ram but allowed Jesus, his Only Son, to die. What really bothers me is that it is clear that God abhorred human sacrifice[42] so why would God test Abraham in this manner? I think Abraham was willing to follow God's command but I also think he felt it wasn't the right thing to do. And that kind of thinking, if I'm correct, is what God was really looking for and found in Abraham.

The second incident is found throughout the Bible and I would have to change the entire story of the Bible if I wanted things my

---

[40] Genesis 22:10

[41] Genesis 22:12

[42] Leviticus 20:1-5

way. I have no intention of changing the story. I just don't have a clear understanding of why things went the way they did. The incident has to do with the Israelites crossing the Jordan River under the leadership of Joshua to take residence in the land God had promised to them. As the story goes, God helped the Israelites defeat those people who were already living in the land. Just to mention one case, after the defeat of Jericho, every living thing in the city was destroyed: *They devoted the city to the LORD and destroyed with the sword every living thing in it — men and women, young and old, cattle, sheep and donkeys.*[43] To devote a city meant to place everything under the curse of death and destruction. In this case, it was Moses who gave this command. But Deuteronomy 20:17 clearly gives God's command and approval to take such action. My problem is this: Why not just go into the land and find places to live, set up the Tabernacle and worship God and begin living the life of a settled holy people as a witness to their faith in God? If the neighboring people made an issue of it and attacked them, then the Israelites had a right to defend themselves, but why go about all the slaughtering to begin with? The Biblical answer is to avoid the temptation of worshiping foreign gods.[44] But consider that during the advent of the Christian era, the disciples were given exactly the opposite orders by Jesus: *Therefore go and make disciples of all nations, baptizing them in the name of the Father and of the Son and of the Holy Spirit, and teaching them to obey everything I have commanded you. And surely I am with you always, to the very end of the age.*[45] He did not say, "Kill everyone around you and take over their land." Although I have to admit, a lot of that did happen when the Church became the dominant faith in the Roman Empire. But my point here is, who would have thought

---

[43] Joshua 6:21
[44] Deuteronomy 20:17-18
[45] Matthew 28:19-20

that those early Christians would one day become such a mighty force in the Empire? Regardless of all this palavering, I still don't understand why anything had to be done the way it was done. I realize I have simplified all this, but we just don't seem to have advanced over the years to any better solution than what Jesus said!

INTRODUCTION
TO BIBLICAL EVIDENCE

What I have done is selected verses from throughout the Bible about fearing God. The verses are grouped in the next section called Biblical Evidence. The verses are not printed out. To have the verses printed out for the reader would be more effective in emphasizing visually the many times fearing God is mentioned, but publishing restraints made it impossible for me to do this. So, find yourself a Bible and read the source material, even some of the larger context. The beauty of having a book like this in digital format is so amazing when you can simply place your computer cursor over the Bible reference to view the translation of your choice! Logos Bible Software offers this with their many Bible programs.[46] You can imagine how convenient such technology is when working with a book such as my book "All the Questions in the Bible" available through Logos.

I have added my personal comments along with each group of verses. My comments are based primarily on the New International Version (NIV), but I also compared other translations and the Hebrew and Greek. In the Bible there are approximately 299 references to fear and 211 references to being afraid; 220 references to terror; 203 references to wrath; and 383 references to anger. For the purposes of this book, I'm mainly concerned with the topic of

---

[46] Contact: customerservice@faithlife.com

fearing God as God would have us to fear him. The Bible gives us a clear picture that God doesn't give up on us. He loves a repentant heart. If you ever feel you're going in the wrong direction, it's never too late to turn around and head back home. My wife was always fond of saying, "You better be prayed up!" Fearing God will help keep us from sinning because the Spirit of God will see our fear as a willingness to follow the ways of God and God will give us his grace to make right choices.

The Scriptures I have selected to comment on are presented in 94 groups and each one contains a verse or verses that mention fearing God. The groups are numbered and just below each number are theme reminders adapted from the Scripture selections. I then list the selected Scripture for you to read prior to reading my brief comments. I also have listed all the Scripture selections together along with the themes at the beginning for an overall look and evaluation.

BIBLICAL EVIDENCE
Selected Verses about Fearing God

SCRIPTURE REFERENCES	GENERAL THEMES
1. Genesis 20:11	No fear of God in this place
2. Genesis 22:12	Now I know that you fear God
3. Genesis 31:42	The God of Abraham and the fear of Isaac
4. Genesis 42:18-19	Do this and you will live, for I fear God
5. Exodus 1:15-17, 21	Because they feared God, he gave them families
6. Exodus 9:15-16, 19-21, 27-30	But I know you still do not fear God
7. Exodus 14:29-31	They feared the Lord and put their trust in him
8. Exodus 18:20-21	Select trustworthy men who fear God
9. Exodus 20:18-20	The fear of God will keep you from sinning
10. Leviticus 19:14 (See 25:17-19, 36, 43)	Fear your God
11. Deuteronomy 5:29, 32-33	Be inclined to fear me
12. Deuteronomy 6:1-3	Fear the Lord your God and enjoy long life
13. Deuteronomy 6:13-16	Fear the Lord your God and serve him only
14. Deuteronomy 6:24-25	Fear the Lord our God and prosper
15. Deuteronomy 10:12-13	Fear the Lord your God and serve him
16. Deuteronomy 10:20-21	Fear the Lord your God and praise him
17. Deuteronomy 25:17-19	They had no fear of God
18. Deuteronomy 31:12-13	Listen and learn to fear the Lord your God
19. Joshua 4:23-24	Always fear the Lord your God

1

~No fear of God in this place~

READ GENESIS 20:11

Comment:

This verse mentions the absence of fear toward God which is what Abraham thought about King Abimelech when traveling through his territory. But Abraham was mistaken about King Abimelech. God actually spoke with King Abimelech in a dream. Fearing God is to have a proper respect toward God but it is much more than just respect. It's knowing that respect means obedience to God and that disrespect brings God's judgment. Therefore, to have no fear of God is to exercise the freedom of doing what one pleases without any responsibility toward God. Such a decision is not a good choice. Whenever you commit a sin—when you act in a manner that displeases God—it proves you do not fear God by your actions at that time.

2

~Now I know that you fear God~

READ GENESIS 22:12

Comment:

This verse is from Genesis, Chapter 22, the story of Abraham being tested by God, about which I have already made some remarks. Fearing God, Abraham was in the process of obeying God's instructions to offer his only son Isaac as a sacrificial burnt offering. As harsh as that may sound, Abraham feared that God would be displeased with him if he did not obey and yet trusted that God could raise Isaac from death.[47] Abraham's wife Sarah had a different experience with fear. When she overheard the Lord telling Abraham that she would bear a child in her old age, she laughed. When challenged: *Sarah was afraid, so she lied and said, I did not laugh. But he said, Yes, you did laugh.*[48] When the child was born, Abraham, who had also laughed[49] named him Isaac which means "he laughs". Sarah then proclaimed: *God has brought me*

---

[47] Genesis 22:8 (See also Hebrews 11:17-19)
[48] Genesis 18:15
[49] Genesis 17:17

laughter, and everyone who hears about this will laugh with me.[50] So, at first Sarah's fear was based on her disbelief whereas later she expressed her fear as laughter in terms of joy and fulfillment toward God. She realized God was right after all!

---

[50] Genesis 21: 6-7 (The Jewish Study Bible edited by Adele Berlin and Marc Zvi Brettler [New York: Oxford University Press, 2004, page 39] points out that in Genesis 18:13 the Lord quotes Sarah emphasizing her old age whereas she had previously in verse 12 emphasized Abraham's old age! The reference says, "The LORD's citation to Abraham of Sarah's monologue in the preceding verse is not quite accurate (*old as I am* as opposed to *with my husband so old*)." Also, "'Great is peace,' remarks a rabbi in the Talmud about this point, 'for even the Holy One (blessed be He) made a change on account of it,' sparing the couple the discord that might have come had Abraham known Sarah's true thought (b. B.M. 87a)." All very interesting, but I see no need for the excitement. Sarah certainly emphasized her own age in verse 12 when she mentioned that she herself was "withered" (TANAKH Translation); "worn out" (NIV); "waxed old" (KJV)!

3

~The God of Abraham and
the Fear of Isaac~

READ GENESIS 31:42

Comment:

Jacob had served Laban for twenty years and is now obeying God's command to return to his homeland with his family and possessions he has accumulated under hardship over the years. Jacob reminds Laban, who is unhappy with the arrangements, that had God not been with him (Jacob), he (Laban) would have sent him away without anything. The Complete Jewish Bible[51] has: *If the God of my father, the God of Avraham, the one who Yitz'chak fears, had not been on my side, by now you would certainly have already sent me away with nothing! God has seen how distressed I've been and how hard I've worked, and last night he passed judgment in my favor.* The Catholic Study Bible[52] translates: *If my ancestral God, the God of Abraham and the Awesome One of Isaac, had not been on my side, you would now have sent me away empty-handed. But God saw my plight and the fruits of my toil, and last night he*

---

51 Translation by David H. Stern
52 The New American Bible translation

gave judgment. The Promise Study Bible[53] translates: *If the fearsome God worshiped by Abraham and my father Isaac had not been on my side, you would have sent me away without a thing. But God saw my hard work, and he knew the trouble I was in, so he helped me. Then last night he told you how wrong you were.* Normally, people fear their enemies, not their friends. It appears that God is only the enemy to those who do not fear him. Fearful reverence and awe include feelings of fear, reverence, and wonder usually caused by something holy and sacred.

---

[53] The Contemporary English Version translation

4

~Do this and you will live, for I fear God~

READ GENESIS 42:18-19

Comment:

These verses are part of the dialogue between Joseph and his brothers in Egypt. Joseph has yet to declare who he is. His brothers are obviously in fear for their lives. Joseph makes known to them that he fears God which actually is a declaration of his belief in the God of his father Jacob. The brothers should have recognized the phrase *I fear God* but probably missed it since Joseph was using a translator. To me personally, the phrase actually becomes a kind of code word for those who worship the Lord God. The sign of the fish became a code for early Christians. Baptism, Communion, the Cross and the name of Jesus are certainly relevant binding modern-day declarations of a Christian witness. We should add to our list, I fear God.

5

~Because they feared God, he gave them families~

READ EXODUS 1:15-17, 21

Comment:

Pharaoh had given an order to the midwives that when helping the Hebrew women during childbirth, the boy children were to be killed. But the midwives feared God more than they feared Pharaoh. They allowed the boy children to live. Notice how God was kind to the midwives and rewarded them. Did you ever wonder if the midwives were Hebrew women or Egyptians?[54] The *Jewish Study Bible* points out: (1) That Pharaoh's scheme to slow down the Hebrew birthrate was interrupted by women—Moses' mother, his sister, the midwives, and Pharaoh's daughter and (2) That Pharaoh wanted to drown Moses but ended up himself in the Red Sea.

---

[54] The Hebrew can read "Hebrew midwives" or "midwives to the Hebrews". Josephus says they were Egyptian. I think they were Hebrew because both names are Semitic. Reference *The Encyclopedia of Jewish Women* on the Web.

6

~*But I know you still do not fear God*~

READ EXODUS 9:15-16, 19-21, 27-30

Comment:

Some things that God can do are really frightening. This kind of fear may be what is mentioned about the officials of Pharaoh who really were afraid of what might come about. Moses promised Pharaoh that the thunder and hail would cease, but he knew that Pharaoh would not keep his promise to let the Israelites depart. He knew this because even though Pharaoh had confessed his sins, admitted that the Lord was right, that his people were wrong, and he had asked for prayer be made to the Lord, Moses knew that Pharaoh and his officials did not fear the Lord God. No real, true belief exists apart from this kind of fear toward God which generates genuine faith and obedience.

7

~They feared the Lord and put their trust in him~

READ EXODUS 14:29-31

Comment:

This fear toward God by the Israelites followed the miraculous crossing of the Red Sea. This great event of separating the waters to allow the safe crossing by the Israelites and then allowing the waters to flow back upon the Egyptians as they tried to cross, became a part of Israel's national heritage uniting fear of God with trust in God. But there were setbacks. The Psalmist wrote: *They forgot the God who saved them, who had done great things in Egypt, miracles in the land of Ham and awesome deeds by the Red Sea.*[55] Jesus said: *You will be hated by everyone because of me, but the one who stands firm to the end will be saved.*[56]

---

[55] Psalm 106:21-22
[56] Matthew 10:22

8

~Select trustworthy men who fear God~

READ EXODUS 18:20-21

Comment:

Moses' father-in-law gave him sound advice in governing the people. First, he reminded him to be a good teacher of all the decrees they were to obey and duties they were to perform. Second, he advised him to be their representative and bring their requests before God. Third, he told Moses to be the judge over difficult cases and appoint capable men to act as judges over other issues. These appointed judges were to be honest and trustworthy men who feared God. I think these officials were people known to Moses who displayed their obedience to the law, their trustworthiness, and their honesty as evidence of their belief and trust in God, and in their fear of God's holiness. When we fear God, we know that God holds us accountable for our behavior.

9

~The fear of God will keep you from sinning~

READ EXODUS 20:18-20

Comment:

At Mount Sinai, the Israelites were terrified at the display of God's mighty power. Introduced here is the idea of (1) being afraid of God because of what they were experiencing in the presence of God and (2) learning to fear God for the purpose of being faithful to him. Moses told the people not to be afraid. This is different from fearing God. Fear of God involves obedience to what God wants accomplished resulting in lives that become holy as God is holy, with the purpose to keep them from sinning. When we sin, it is obvious that we do not take God seriously. When we truly fear God, we are conscious of his majesty and power and it becomes paramount in our minds that sin offends him.

10

~*Fear your God*~

READ LEVITICUS 19:14
(SEE ALSO LEVITICUS 25:17-19, 36, 43)

Comment:

In the midst of many laws and rules is this reminder to *fear your God*, followed by *I am the LORD*. This combination of reminder and declaration could easily be added to every law and rule listed![57] Christians often speak against using curse words but fail to see that putting an obstacle in front of a blind person is also a means of cursing without saying a word! We are simply not to take advantage of one another. I like what the Zondervan Bible Commentary says about cursing the deaf: "...they could not hear the cursing! But God would hear, and he is the Protector of the unfortunate."

---

[57] See also Deuteronomy 27 and 28:15-68

11

~Be inclined to fear me~

READ DEUTERONOMY 5:29, 32-33

Comment:

Moses is relating to the Israelites what the Lord told him to say to them. God was pleased with how the people had previously responded to Moses and now God's desire is that they would be inclined to fear God and obey his commands. Their fearing God and their obedience to God's commands are always connected. It's understandable to see this fear connection in terms of endearment and reverence, but the term fear must also carry with it the idea that this is a serious desire and commitment of the deepest possible promise. Following the ways of God is not a game. And even if it were, we don't make the rules to play by. We are to listen carefully and do what God wants done.

12

~Fear the Lord your God and enjoy long life~

READ DEUTERONOMY 6:1-3

Comment:

Moses is telling the Israelites that the commands, decrees, and laws he is teaching them are directly from God and meant for their good. They are reminded to be careful in obedience that all may go well with them. It's interesting to me that although there is much said in this chapter about the mighty power of God, the first twelve verses speak only about loving God and being faithful to him. To fear God in love is not to see him as a threat but as someone who loves and cares. We see this more clearly with the coming of the Messiah Jesus who said: *I have come that they may have life, and have it to the full.*[58]

---

[58] John 10:10

13

~Fear the Lord your God and serve him only~

READ DEUTERONOMY 6:13-16

Comment:

We find here a very good reason why we should fear God as well as adore him. This verse tells us that God is a jealous God. One of the names of God is "Jealous": *Do not worship any other god, for the LORD, whose name is Jealous, is a jealous God.*[59] When God spoke to Moses on Mount Sinai, the very first commandment he gave him was not to have any other gods.[60] Why? Because there are no other living gods. The other so-called gods are fashioned from wood or stone and cannot hear, eat, smell, speak, see, feel, or walk: *Those who make them will be like them, and so will all who trust in them.*[61]

---

[59] Exodus 34:14
[60] Exodus 20:1-3
[61] Deuteronomy 4:28 and Psalm 115:2-8

14

~*Fear the Lord our God and prosper*~

READ DEUTERONOMY 6:24-25

Comment:

Fearing God secures our prosperity and provides our righteousness through our obedience to his commands. God alone has the righteousness we need to survive. There are Christian ministers who actually preach a prosperity gospel, a theology which sees faith in God delivering security and prosperity. This is not what is meant in these verses about prospering. God's commands about how to live are not meant to make everyone who follows them rich and famous! They are meant to make life itself rich in living. Jesus said: *What good is it for a man to gain the whole world, yet forfeit his soul? Or what can a man give in exchange for his soul?*[62]

---

[62] Mark 8:36-37

15

~Fear the Lord your God and serve him~

READ DEUTERONOMY 10:12-13

Comment:

This verse alone explains in detail what it means to fear the Lord our God. This kind of fear is not fright. If we are ever afraid of God, we probably deserve it! We must not ever think that God is just going to overlook our faults. It would not benefit us. He's there to help us, not punish us. To fear God is knowing that God alone has what we need to survive and that without him we are lost. It is complete devotion to God, walking in all his ways, loving him and serving him with all our heart and soul.

16

~Fear the Lord your God and praise him~

READ DEUTERONOMY 10:20-21

Comment:

If nothing else, we should fear the loss of God, for without him we are without hope. To have his continued love and grace, power and wonders, we need to hold fast to him whose name is to be everlastingly praised. If you don't believe in God, there's no God to fear and also no God to praise. You can't even say "God bless you" when someone sneezes. Did you know that the phrase "God bless you" came out of the Middle Ages and the bubonic plague? According to my information, fits of sneezing indicated death was near, so people would say, "God bless you".[63]

---

[63] Bill McLain, *Do Fish Drink Water?* (New York: MJF Books, 1999) p. 109.

17

~*They had no fear of God*~

READ DEUTERONOMY 25:19

Comment:

The Amalekites were bitter enemies of the Israelites from the time they left Egypt even to the time of Kings Saul and David. The Amalekites became a symbol of evil who, displaying no fear of God, attempted to destroy God's people. I have already mentioned my thoughts about the actions God wanted the Israelites to take against their enemies, and these verses about the Amalekites are just another reminder of what was expected to take place: *When the LORD your God gives you rest from all the enemies around you in the land he is giving you to possess as an inheritance, you shall blot out the name of Amalek from under heaven. Do not forget!*[64]

---

[64] Deuteronomy 25:19

18

~Listen and learn to fear the Lord your God~

READ DEUTERONOMY 31:12-13

Comment:

Moses commanded the priests and elders of Israel to listen and learn and follow carefully all the words of the law. It must not be neglected, especially for the children who did not know the law. It took place in the family gatherings and in the teaching sessions of the priests.[65] Learning to fear God was to be instructed in the righteousness of God. Foreigners were also included. My first introduction to attending Church began when I was about 10 years of age. A lady from the First Baptist Church of Belton, South Carolina came to my home and asked my mother if she would allow me to attend Sunday School at the Church. My mother agreed and my life was set in motion to guide me toward my pursuit in life of becoming a Christian minister. I loved going to Church from the very beginning. The hot dog suppers certainly helped to hold my attention, but I enjoyed the company of other

---

[65] In the Temple in Jerusalem when Jesus was twelve years of age, he was found by his parents *sitting among the teachers, listening to them and asking them questions* (see Luke 2:41-51).

boys and girls my age, learning about Jesus, and singing songs. There was one song in particular that I've remembered through the years. The song went along with a beautiful picture I remember hanging on the classroom wall. The picture was in color and illustrated a circle of children from around the world dressed in their native costumes. The song lyrics in 1947 were:

> Jesus loves the little children
> All the children of the world
> Red and yellow, black and white
> They are precious in His sight
> Jesus loves the little children of the world.

This was in a small South Carolina town with segregated churches, schools, theaters, and restaurants. I was glad to be one of those children Jesus loved and learned a lot about my faith from singing that song.

19

~Always fear the Lord your God~

READ JOSHUA 4:23-24

Comment:

Understanding the mighty acts of God is important in experiencing the power in fearing God. Studying the Bible is not an option. We have a need to know as much as possible from both the Old Testament and the New Testament. Don't count on Hollywood to get everything right—like the person reading the Bible and saying, "That's not the way it happened. I saw the movie!" Also, it is not enough just to know the stories—not just what the stories say, but what they mean by what they say. And then we have to reform our lives to the lessons we learn: *Do not conform to the pattern of this world, but be transformed by the renewing of your mind.*[66]

---

[66] Romans 12:2

20

~Fear the Lord and serve him in all faithfulness~

READ JOSHUA 24:14-15

Comment:

These words from Joshua come after recounting from the very words of God all the mighty things God had done for his people. Joshua calls for all the people to fear the Lord and in all faithfulness to serve him. To really fear the Lord is to put aside all allegiance to other gods and serve only the Lord God. It is a continuing endeavor that occupies every moment of life which means there are no areas in life that are exempted, no private times to neglect the journey, and no secret compartments that leave God out of your life. And if you choose to serve the Lord, know that he will not take second place in any of your endeavors.

21

~Fear the Lord and do not rebel against him~

READ 1 SAMUEL 12:14-15, 24-25

Comment:

To fear the Lord is to serve him and obey him and not rebel against him. To rebel against the Lord is to assure his hand will be against you rather than for you. Persisting in evil is rebellion against God. Regardless of what impressions I personally might have about some Old Testament stories of crime and punishment, God is still, for me, the absolute epitome of goodness and the enemy of evil. His love is securely sincere. As Romans puts it: *Hate what is evil; cling to what is good.*[67] Also: *Do not be overcome by evil, but overcome evil with good.*[68] And: *Therefore love is the fulfillment of the law.*[69]

---

[67] Romans 12:9
[68] Romans 12:21
[69] Romans 13:10

22

~Rule in the fear of the Lord~

READ 2 SAMUEL 23:2-4

Comment:

These last words of King David reveal the basis of all Godly rulers. They rule in righteousness, in the fear of God. Their fear is grounded in a relationship with God that results in good things for all the people, like the brightness of a sunrise, like raindrops that nourish the earth. I remember from my childhood in South Carolina the adage: "When it's raining and the sun is shining, the devil is beating his wife."[70] Proverbs has a better adage: *When a king's face brightens, it means life; his favor is like a rain cloud in spring*[71]. Also: *A king's rage is like the roar of a lion, but his favor is like dew on the grass.*[72]

---

[70] For more on this idea, see the topic "Sunshower" at Wikipedia on the Web.

[71] Proverbs 16:15 (In my book *A New View of Proverbs*, Section 27, I list 37 Proverbs dealing with the subject of "Leaders and Leadership".)

[72] Proverbs 19:12

23

~Fear the Lord all the time~

READ 1 KINGS 8:39-43
(SEE ALSO 2 CHRONICLES 6:32-33)

Comment:

The fear of God and all its great benefits are extended not only to the Israelites but to everyone throughout the world who will come to God's great Name, his mighty hand, and his outstretched arm. From the very beginning, God promised that everyone would be blessed through the ancestry of Abraham.[73] When Peter was preaching, he proclaimed that what had been foretold through the prophets was fulfilled in the coming of the Messiah Jesus.[74] Jesus said: *Come to me, all you who are weary and burdened, and I will give you rest.*[75]

---

[73] Genesis 12:3
[74] See Acts 3:17-26
[75] Matthew 21:28

24

~He is to be feared above all idols~

READ 1 CHRONICLES 16:25-26, 30

Comment:

These verses contain direct commands for everyone to fear God and tremble before him (a Psalm of David[76]). To fear God is to praise him. What a strange combination—fear and praise. There are other words that have a softer tone: adore and revere are often used and should be. But fear still maintains its status as a dominate fixture in the halls of heaven. When we think about normal fears we face in life, they bring to mind thoughts of an enemy, of facing failure, of uncertain challenges, things definitely out of our comfort zone. But to fear God is to know we are definitely outnumbered but in loving hands.[77]

---

[76] See 1 Chronicles 16:7.

[77] Compare 1 Chronicles 16:8-22 with Psalms 105:1-15; 1 Chronicles 16:23-33 with Psalms 96:1-13; and 1 Chronicles 16:34-36 with Psalms 106:1, 47-48.

25

~Let the fear of the Lord be with you~

2 CHRONICLES 19:7-10

Comment:

The administrators of justice were faithfully and wholeheartedly committed to serving the Lord God, warning the people not to sin against the Lord. Timothy was reminded that: *God's solid foundation stands firm, sealed with this inscription: "The Lord knows those who are his," and, "Everyone who confesses the name of the Lord must turn away from wickedness."*[78] Sometimes just turning away isn't enough. You may have to run away.[79] I remember when fishing in Alaska, I turned away and ran away from the bear that wanted my fish!

---

[78] 2 Timothy 2:19
[79] 2 Timothy 2:22

26

~He was instructed in the fear of the Lord~
READ 2 CHRONICLES 26:3-5

Comment:

The New International Version footnote suggests an alternate reading of "vision" instead of "fear". When "fear of God" includes the idea of seeking to worship and obey him, I personally have no problem with the NIV use of "fear". The King James Version has: *And he sought God in the days of Zechariah, who had understanding in the visions of God: and as long as he sought the LORD, God made him to prosper.* The Jewish Study Bible reads: *He applied himself to the worship of God during the time of Zechariah, instructor in the visions of God; during the time he worshiped the LORD, God made him prosper.* The Jewish Study Bible has a footnote that some Hebrew manuscripts read "fear".

27

~Fear the commands of our God~

READ EZRA 9:3; 10:3

Comment:

The use of the terms *trembled at the words of the God of Israel* and *fear the commands of our God* in these two Ezra passages are not exactly focused on the "fear of God". They are aimed at the fear of the "commands of God". Now, you might ask what difference does it make? To see the difference, in my opinion, you would have to understand their use in the Book of Ezra. The situation concerns the matter of foreign marriages[80] in which preserving a separate people was a major concern, leading to the separation of fear of God (and following God's commands) and unfaithfulness to the commands themselves (without any concern for God's grace). In other words, it's possible in some instances to make the commands of God more important than God himself: "Therefore whatever opinion we may form of the particular action of Ezra, we should do well to ponder gravely over the grand principle on which it was based. God must have the first place in the hearts and lives of His

---

[80] For a review of this problem, see Walter F. Adeney, *The Expositor's Bible: Ezra, Nehemiah, and Esther* (London: Hodder and Stoughton Publishers, Second Edition, 1906). The Book of Esther (8:17) states that *many people of other nationalities became Jews because fear of the Jews had seized them.*

people, even though in some cases this may involve the shipwreck of the dearest earthly affections."[81] I personally do not agree with Ezra's actions concerning the foreign marriages. If the Israelites were wrong in taking foreign wives, then their faith in God should have been their guiding light to redemption. If repentance was in order, then the declaration of wrong-doing should have been made public and grace should have prevailed. When Jesus declared that anyone who loves their father or mother more than him would not be worthy of him, he didn't suggest getting rid of your father and mother.[82]

---

[81] Ibid, p. 152.
[82] Matthew 10:37

28

~Walk in the fear of our God~

READ NEHEMIAH 5:9

Comment:

Harsh economic conditions brought about Nehemiah's anger toward the nobles and officials. It's interesting to note Nehemiah's concern that outsiders would have bad things to say if the Israelites did not walk in the fear of God and not set a good example in dealing with one another. I remember my brother-in-law telling about his employer, a car dealer (and a church deacon) who wanted him to turn back the odometer on a car he, as a mechanic, was preparing for sale. The church deacon was certainly not a very good Christian witness in the conduct of his business practices. The Bible says: *Do not use dishonest standards when measuring length, weight or quantity.*[83]

---

[83] Leviticus 19:35

29

~A man who fears God and shuns evil~

READ JOB 1:8-10; 2:3

Comment:

Satan accused God of surrounding Job's life with so many blessings (the hedge) that Job was obliged to fear God or lose his blessings. But Job did lose his blessings, still feared God, and learned in the end that God's majesty was his everlasting hope. Job's life was filled with suffering and his "friends" accused him of wrongdoing and urged him to confess his sins. Job knew something was terribly wrong behind the scenes. Job grieved for the loss of God's companionship. He also grieved when his "friends" gave him advice. I have a crocheted plaque in my office that reads:

Don't worry about your station in life…
There will always be someone ready
to tell you where to get off!

30

~*Forsaking the fear of the Almighty*~

READ JOB 6:14

Comment:

The updated New International Version has changed their translation of this verse from: *A despairing man should have the devotion of his friends, even though he forsakes the fear of the Almighty* to read: *Anyone who withholds kindness from a friend forsakes the fear of the Almighty.* It isn't Job who has forsaken the fear of the Almighty but his friends who are falsely accusing him. Job's fear of the Almighty is a deep, abiding trust that demands justice and understanding.

31

~*When I think of all this, I fear him*~

READ JOB 23:10-17

Comment:

Job's fear of God is based on his knowledge that God can and does what he pleases. But Job knows that when the testing is done, he will come out in triumph. My first encounter with a major problem as an Air Force Chaplain came very soon after I arrived at my first assignment at Laredo Air Force Base, Texas. A young airman had been severely burned in an accident on the flight line. I stood beside the military doctor as he did what he could to help. Neither prayer nor medical science was enough to save him. That was 51 years ago. I still have trouble understanding people who say and do negative things against our flag and country.

32

~The fear of the Lord – that is wisdom~

READ JOB 28:28

Comment:

To fear God is to keep close to him and avoid evil because God knows what is best. He created everything, knows all and sees all. When thinking about wisdom and understanding, it is only natural to consider the wisdom God gave to King Solomon whom the Bible declares to have possessed wisdom greater than anyone else. He also had more wives than anyone else! His wives, according to the account in 1 Kings, Chapter 11, were instrumental in causing Solomon to turn away from full devotion to the Lord God. He failed to keep God's commands. Solomon's following the path of evil ways brought about God's anger toward him. Solomon did not fear God's clear instructions to shun evil. He was rich in gold, wise in judgment, but poor in fear of God.

33

~For fear of his splendor I could not do such things~

READ JOB 31:23

Comment:

Job recounts the many injustices he could not inflict upon others, knowing such actions would not reflect the goodness of God in his life. The grandeur of God prevented him from doing what he knew was displeasing to God. Yet, Job finds himself shadowed by the (he believes) apparent absence of God in his life. He can get no clear answers from anyone (even God) as to the reason for all his suffering. He does not discard his believing in God. He desires to have an audience before God to understand what is going on. He will get this desire of his heart. God will finally reveal himself to Job in a manner that Job does not expect. In the end, Job is totally surprised by the grandeur and majesty of God. He sees behind the scene that God is right about everything.

34

~Serve and celebrate the Lord with fear and trembling~

READ PSALM 2:11

Comment:

Serving God with fear and celebrating his rule with trembling, in my opinion, is both emotional and downright smart. I'm reminded that the idea of reverence toward God is often associated with the idea of fear toward God. The main thing to keep in mind is that as Christians we should always at all times resist the idea that we are equal with God: *For my thoughts are not your thoughts, neither are your ways my ways, declares the LORD.*[84] Read the Doxology in Romans 11:33-36. We humans keep discovering new things. Some of us keep forgetting what we have learned. What is it that God does so people will fear him? Read Ecclesiastes 3:14-15. Fear and trembling will keep you in the right frame of mind to please God.

---

[84] Isaiah 55:8

35

~Honor those who fear the Lord~

READ PSALM 15:1-5

Comment:

I have gotten comments from people throughout my career as a minister and chaplain stating we continue to be sinners even after becoming saved and baptized. I think they mean to imply that we should not worry much about sinning after we become converted, which I believe is wrong. It is true that we can still sin after conversion. As my mother used to say jokingly about baptism: "They are dry sinners when they go down into the water and wet sinners when they come out!" We should always try to do what is right in the eyes of God! He observes us at all times: *His eyes are on the ways of mortals; he sees their every step.*[85]

---

[85] Job 34:21.

36

~The fear of the Lord is pure,
enduring forever~

READ PSALM 19:9

Comment:

In Psalm 19, fear of the Lord is listed as one of six great concepts of the Lord; the other five are: the law of the Lord which refreshes our soul; the statutes of the Lord which give us wisdom; the precepts of the Lord which give joy to our heart; the commands of the Lord which give light to our eyes; and the decrees of the Lord which warn us and which bring us great reward when we keep them. The Psalm ends with: *May the words of my mouth and this meditation of my heart be pleasing in your sight, LORD, my Rock and my Redeemer.*[86] The fear of the Lord is listed as pure and enduring forever. It is what keeps us faithful in obedience to all that pleases God. It is not a fleeting emotional trait; it is forever a glorious endeavor.

---

[86] Psalm 19:14

37

~If you fear the Lord: praise, honor, and revere him~

READ PSALM 22:23-25

Comment:

In this translation, note that "fear" is used twice and "revere" once, a combination of reverence, worship and obedience, as brought out in the entire Psalm.[87] From the Cross, Jesus quoted the first verse of this Psalm: *My God, my God, why have you forsaken me?* We don't know, but Jesus could have recited from memory the entire Psalm which ends with:

> *Posterity will serve him;*
> *Future generations will be told about the Lord.*
> *They will proclaim his righteousness,*
> *Declaring to a people yet unborn:*
> *He has done it!*[88]

---

[87] See *A Handbook on Psalms* by Robert G. Bratcher and William D. Reyburn (New York: United Bible Societies), pages 224-226.
[88] Psalm 22:30-31

38

~God will instruct those who fear him~

READ PSALM 25:4-5, 12-14

Comment:

In understanding fear toward God, it involves more than lighting a candle, or making the sign of the cross, or kneeling. It is a daily dependence on God for forgiveness, guidance, and love. It is knowing that God takes notice and reveals himself to us. There was a time when being known was hard to come by. Not anymore! Now it's hard not to be noticed! Cameras are everywhere. I have cameras watching anyone approaching my front or back door. I live in Florida and can check out my son's farm in Ohio. The Bible tells us that: *The eyes of the LORD are everywhere, keeping watch on the wicked and the good.*[89] Good or bad, we all need his instruction in righteousness.

---

[89] Proverbs 15:3

39

~You store up goodness for those who fear you~

READ PSALM 31:19

Comment:

Here we have fear of God in the sense of taking refuge in him. Notice that God's goodness is both stored up and bestowed that everyone may see how great God is to all who depend on him. Here again it is clear that this kind of fear is not meant to drive people away from God. It is a relationship with God that consists of abundant good from God. It is so much good, so much overflowing that it has to be stored up for distribution to those who seek him! In the context of this Psalm, God provides such things as trust, hope, love, truthfulness, and mercy to those who seek shelter in his presence. One of my very favorite verses is verse 15: *My times are in your hands.*

40

~*His eyes are on those who fear him*~

READ PSALM 33:8, 18-22

Comment:

Fearing the Lord involves revering the Lord; putting our hope in his unfailing love to help us and shield us; trusting in his holy name with joyful hearts. I've met people who said they believed in God but seldom do I hear people say they hope in his unfailing love in times of distress or who rejoice in trusting in his care. When we fear God we acknowledge his love for us and his desire for us to make good choices in life. And he will help us to do just that. Ask God for help. Talk to him. It doesn't have to be a formal type of prayer. Read the Bible daily. Be thankful for his blessings. Live under his watchful eyes: *Turn from evil and do good; seek peace and pursue it.*[90]

---

[90] Psalm 34:14

41

*~The Lord's angel encamps
around those who fear him~*

READ PSALM 34:7-11

Comment:

In David's Psalm 34, fearing God is mentioned four times. The entire chapter reveals much about what it means to fear God, as we are invited to learn in verse 11. Read the entire chapter carefully and notice the parallelism in each verse. Note the many themes: extol and praise; boast, hear and rejoice; glorify and exalt, sought, answered, and delivered; look and faces; called, heard and saved; the Lord's Angel who encamps around and delivers; taste, see, and take refuge; love life and desire good days; speak no evil, turn from evil; do good and seek peace; know that the Lord is attentive to those who need him and against those who do wrong; he is a friend to the brokenhearted and those crushed in spirit; taking refuge in the Lord brings redemption.

42

~There is no fear of God before the eyes of the wicked~

READ PSALM 36:1-4

Comment:

If you have any problem trying to understand what it means to fear God, at least you have this verse which explains quite clearly what it means not to fear God.[91] Then all you have to do is turn everything around in favor of fearing God! That would mean to have the fear of God before your eyes and hate sin. Not just to hate sin but to hate your sin (verse 2). Keep your thoughts wise and strive always to speak gloriously of God and to do good at all times. Pray and commit yourself to a righteous course that rejects all wrong. Seriously ask yourself: Do I fear God? Say to yourself: I don't fear God. What's your answer to the question? Then, how do you feel when say you don't fear God?

---

[91] See also Romans 3:18

43

~See, fear, praise, and put your trust in the Lord~

READ PSALM 40:3-8

Comment:

Fear and trust. Fearing God brings praise and a desire to do his will. When I put my trust in him, I am doing so because I've been invited to see him. I fear him because he is above me, beyond me, and yet all around me and in me, in my heart. And now I trust him and desire to do his will. I have listened to song writers as they explain how a new hit tune came into being. I'm always amazed that in one special moment of time there came into being a word or two, a lyric, a tune, and eventually a hit song that sold millions of copies! Sometimes a song will do poorly when sung by one artist and then burst into "fame" when sung by another! It's always a hit when God puts: *a new song in my mouth, a hymn of praise to our God.*

44

~The righteous will see, fear and laugh~

READ PSALM 52:6-7

Comment:

Jesus said: *But blessed are your eyes because they see, and your ears because they hear. For truly I tell you, many prophets and righteous people longed to see what you see but did not see it, and to hear what you hear but did not hear it.*[92] To see and fear and laugh is to observe and choose the right pathway, trusting God and making him your stronghold. To "laugh at" is not to make fun of but to express amazement at what happens to someone who does not depend on God.

---

[92] Matthew 13:16-17

45

~He raises a banner for those who fear him~

READ PSALM 60:4-5, 12

Comment:

This entire Chapter is difficult to understand. The Psalmist is again seeking God's help and expects victory (verses 5 and 12). But it appears that the Israelites are being defeated in battle and they want God to help things go their way toward victory. God has provided a sign of hope (banner) to show those who fear him (those he loves) that he will protect them from the enemy (bow and arrows). Maybe the banner is simply God's way of letting them know that in spite of defeat, he will be with them in their recovering from the disaster. It is quite clear that without God's help no victory for the Israelites is possible: *Give us aid against the enemy, for human help is worthless* (verse 11).

46

*~Those who fear God's name
have a heritage~*

READ PSALM 61:2-5

Comment:

This Psalm has the beautiful prayer: *...lead me to the rock that is higher than I.* This rock is a strong and safe place to protect us from harm's way. Paul wrote about his ancestors who drank from the spiritual rock that was Christ.[93] There is mention of a heritage of those who fear God's name. I take the idea of heritage to mean that God has given everyone who fears him a place to dwell together in peace. Jesus said: *You believe in God; believe also in me. My Father's house has many rooms; if that were not so, would I have told you that I am going there to prepare a place for you?*[94]

---

[93] 1 Corinthians 10:1-4
[94] John 14:1-2

47

~Tell those who fear the Lord what he has done for you~

READ PSALM 66:16

Comment:

My first reaction to this verse was why tell what God has done for me just to those who fear him? Feel free to tell others about your faith even when they disagree, but feel assured that others who fear the Lord will welcome your testimony! Regardless, make sure you know what God has done for you. In the midst of my loneliness he has sent me friends; in the midst of my doubts he has directed me to sources of truth; in the midst of my sins he has reminded me of a better way; in the midst of my weakness he has strengthened my spirit. Jesus said: *Come to me, all you who are weary and burdened, and I will give you rest.*[95]

---

[95] Matthew 11:28

48

~It is you alone who are to be feared~

READ PSALM 76:7-12

Comment:

Fear toward God has to contend with his power to create and destroy. His power is also a liberating force bringing praise from the afflicted. We fear God, knowing he is in charge of all that is good in life and we don't want to be separated from his goodness. We know the depth of his love which drives out all other fear.[96] Our goodness is derived from God's gracious love to us and our decision to accept Him, honor Him, and live forever with Him: *And this is the testimony: God has given us eternal life, and this life is in his Son. Whoever has the Son has life; whoever does not have the Son of God does not have life.*[97]

---

[96] See 1 John 4:18
[97] 1 John 5:11-12

49

~Teach me, Lord, that I may fear your name~

READ PSALM 86:11

Comment:

Ask the Lord to teach you his way. Then walk in his truth. Ask him to give you an undivided heart that puts him always in first place. Then you will have no problem fearing God. Jesus said: *Do not be afraid of those who kill the body but cannot kill the soul. Rather, be afraid of the One who can destroy both soul and body in hell.*[98] The soul is not immortal without a spiritual rebirth. Now, fearing God's name is another matter. God's name itself is a topic too vast to treat here. God's name soon became unpronounceable from the earliest of times for fear that it would be taken in vain and therefore violate one of the Ten Commandments. That has always puzzled me because if you can't pronounce God's name, how can you praise his name? And if you use another name, there is always the possibility of that name being taken in vain. If you're interested in a journey in the direction of God's name, do some research, even on the Internet, on the word "tetragrammaton". Now, about the undivided heart. Jesus said: *No one can serve two*

---

[98] Matthew 10:28 (See also Luke 12:5)

masters. Either you will hate the one and love the other, or you will be devoted to the one and despise the other. You cannot serve both God and money.[99] You cannot split up your loyalty to God. Not even 99% for God and 1% for someone else. God requires a particular type of loyalty that is either for him or against him. Again, Jesus said: *Whoever is not with me is against me, and whoever does not gather with me scatters.*[100] If you're traveling and come to a split in the road, you can't drive in two directions at the same time. If God is the way you want to go, the commitment must be 100%. Better to rely on God's help and ask him to teach you his way.

---

[99] Matthew 6:24
[100] Mathew 12:30

50

~God is greatly feared by all who surround him~

READ PSALM 89:5-8, 47

Comment:

These verses should be read along with Psalm 19:1 which reads: *The heavens declare the glory of God; the skies proclaim the work of his hands.* There is no one greater than God. When the Psalmist realizes the eternal greatness of God, his primary thought to God about himself is: *Remember how fleeting is my life.*[101] The word "fleeting" means to pass by swiftly. The Bible tells us that to God a day is like a thousand years, and a thousand years are like a day.[102] Whatever that means, it's certainly beyond my way of counting! But the older I get, my years do seem to pass a bit faster. I can't imagine how to count eternity!

---

[101] Psalm 89:47
[102] 2 Peter 3:8

51

~Your wrath is as great as the fear that is your due~

READ PSALM 90:7-12

Comment:

Verse 11 about fear has many possible translations. I take the fear mentioned to include the knowledge of God's power which must also include the power of his wrath. To avoid any wrath of God there must be a turning away from any wrong doing. We must learn from our fear of God that our days are numbered and we must be governed by his wisdom.[103] As I write these comments, I remember celebrating my 82ⁿᵈ Birthday just 5 days ago. As of today, I have lived 29,955 days! If I slept an average of 8 hours per day, I have spent 9,985 days sleeping! May we use our time wisely! These verses tell us that our days may come to seventy years or maybe eighty if we're able to handle it, and then we fly away![104] I think I'm on borrowed time!

---

[103] See Psalm 111:10
[104] Psalm 90:10

52

~The Lord's love is with those who fear him~

READ PSALM 103:11-18

Comment:

Those who fear God and keep God's covenant and obey his precepts are recipients of God's love, forgiveness, and compassion. God's love is as great as the heavens are high. He has removed our transgressions out of reach—as far as the east is from the west. We are also told in this Psalm that while life on earth may fade like the flowers, God's love is from everlasting to everlasting with those who fear him. I know it sounds strange to have fear toward someone who loves you, but God's love and holiness, and concern, and compassion, and righteousness, and forgiveness is all so overwhelming and gracious that to stand before him in awe and reverence is to fear the very ground we stand on and to fear God himself: *For God so loved the world that he gave his one and only Son, that whoever believes in him shall not perish but have eternal life.*[105]

---

[105] John 3:16

53

~Blessed are those who fear the Lord~

READ PSALM 112:1

Comment:

Fear toward God actually brings the blessing of delight (great joy in his commands) in doing God's will. Luke's Gospel tells of a centurion who sent for Jesus to heal his servant who was very sick. While Jesus was on his way he was met by more messengers who related that the centurion felt unworthy for Jesus to enter his home and wanted him to simply issue a command for his servant to be healed, explaining that as a centurion he understood the power of a command. When the messengers returned to the house, they found the servant healed. Jesus is reported as saying: *I tell you, I have not found such great faith even in Israel.*[106] There is power in all Jesus says.

---

[106] Luke 7:1-10

54

~Fear the Lord and proclaim
His enduring love~

READ PSALM 118:4

Comment:

To fear God is to have an enduring love for the Lord and to know that God has an enduring love for you. It's interesting that Verse 6 of this Psalm says: *The LORD is with me; I will not be afraid.* When we fear the Lord, we will not be afraid! It could be that we have every right to fear God, knowing that he is capable of inflicting upon us whatever he desires. But what we realize when we get to know him is a dear helpful friend who has no intention of harming us. I watched as our neighbor's child grew up playing alongside their Rottweiler pet in their fenced back yard. The dog never liked me. But there was never any problem between the child and the dog. I outlived the dog. I'm sorry, but I don't miss him. The young child is now a lovely young girl.

55

~Those who fear God have a mutual understanding~

READ PSALM 119:38, 63, 74, 79, 120

Comment:

Psalm 119 is the longest of the 150 Psalms. The Psalm's theme is about the joy of observing God's Law. The Psalm has 22 divisions each containing 8 verses for a total of 176 verses. In the Hebrew text, each of the verses in each of the 22 divisions begin with the corresponding letter of the 22 letters of the Hebrew alphabet, from the first letter Aleph to the last letter Taw. These letters of the Hebrew Alphabet are listed in the New International Version (and other versions) at the beginning of each division. Also, eight words normally associated with the Law are mentioned in the Psalm: (1) Law; (2) Testimony; (3) Judgment; (4) Commandment; (5) Decree (Statutes); (6) Precepts; (7) Word; (8) Promises. It could be said when looking at the verse references chosen for this Group relating to fearing God that standing in awe of God's laws is the same as fearing God, but the Psalmist fears God, not just the laws. Of course, one can also stand in awe of God which is included with anyone fearing God. But notice that he also trembles! In Psalm 119:38 there is a request for God to fulfill a promise made so God may be feared. Fulfillment of promises establishes for the Psalmist recognition of God's majesty. In Psalm 130:3-4 the Psalmist is hoping that God doesn't keep a record of sins because no one would be able to stand. He concludes that with God there is forgiveness and therefore God can be served in reverence. The King James Version has fear instead of reverence.

56

~Fear and praise the Lord~

READ PSALM 135:19-21

Comment:

The Psalmist calls upon three groups to praise the Lord: (1) All the Israelites; (2) the house of Aaron (the priests); (3) the house of Levi (keepers of the Temple). The critical part is that whatever group you are from, you must fear God which means there is no idolatry in your heart. The Lord from Zion is the God of all Israel represented by the Temple in Jerusalem. And he is to be praised by everyone who dwells in Jerusalem. The Temple no longer exists but God has not gone away. He is still very much in control of his creation and still welcomes our utmost attention, our fear of his majesty and the heartfelt praise of everyone throughout the world.

57

~God fulfills the desires of those who fear Him~

READ PSALM 145:19

Comment:

It is not enough just to desire the Lord. To call on him is to approach him in truth—to desire his ways in fear of his holiness. The Lord desires for us to come to him in repentance and be willing to be obedient to him. It is not his will that anyone should perish.[107] We must come to him with full assurance of his dominance in power, knowledge and presence. We must fear his majesty, knowing that he is loving, kind, forgiving, and filled with compassion regarding our human existence, ready to take our weakness and turn it into strength and lead us into his world of righteousness. When we truly desire him, he will hear our cries and save us.

---

[107] 2 Peter 3:9

58

~The Lord delights in those who fear Him~

READ PSALM 147:11

Comment:

In this verse we learn that the Lord himself delights in those who fear him, who put their hope in his unfailing love. How can I fear someone who loves me? Well, I may have doubts if someone tells me they love me or I may even fear that my response to someone's love is not genuine. How many love stories and romantic movies reveal love as twisted, torn, and broken? How many people enter into marriage fearing they have made a mistake? Fearing God is dealing in eternal hope with the unknown revealed: *Now faith is confidence in what we hope for and assurance about what we do not see.*[108]

---

[108] Hebrews 11:1

59

~The fear of the Lord is the beginning of knowledge~

READ PROVERBS 1:7, 28-31

Comment:

To fear the Lord is to know he is holy and does not condone sin. Fools are those individuals inclined to do evil. Fear of God brings the very presence of God's Spirit who grants wisdom and knowledge which leads to the ability to make good choices in life and to exhibit good behavior. For those who choose not to fear God, they are like those spoken of by the Prophet Isaiah...*who did not look to the One who made it, or have regard for the one who planned it long ago.*[109] Those who choose not to fear God are given this ultimatum: *Then they will call to me but I will not answer; they will look for me but will not find me, since they hated knowledge and did not choose to fear the LORD.* (verses 28-29)

---

[109] Isaiah 22:11

60

~Understanding the fear of the Lord~

READ PROVERBS 2:1-6

Comment:

Even as our faith is a gift from God,[110] the same is true about fearing the Lord. We understand the fear of the Lord when we accept his words, storing up his commands within us, listening to his wisdom, applying our hearts (lives), yearning and desiring earnestly to understand his ways, searching for God's wisdom as we would search for precious stones and treasures. In return, God gives us freely the ability to possess his wisdom and obtain the necessary fear that captivates our lives and motivates us to serve God in holiness. Fearing the Lord is more than just standing before him in awe and admiration. It is an intimate relationship with God that puts us out of our normal comfort zone.

---

[110] Ephesians 2:8-10

61

~Fear the Lord and shun evil~

READ PROVERBS 3:5-8

Comment:

In Genesis 2, God had told Adam not to eat from the tree of the knowledge of good and evil. In Genesis 3, the serpent informed Eve that eating from the tree would result in knowing good and evil. In seeking serpent-gained wisdom, Eve (and Adam) disobeyed God. God always knows best. It is always best for us to trust in the Lord and stop relying on our own wisdom to discern what is right and wrong. When we acknowledge God, he will grant us the fear and the wisdom necessary to direct us to what is right. Proverbs 3 is a good starting place to begin learning what is right: *Trust in the LORD with all your heart and lean not on your own understanding; in all your ways submit to him, and he will make your paths straight.* (verses 5-6)

62

~To fear the Lord is to hate evil~

READ PROVERBS 8:13

Comment:

Jesus said: *For it is from within, out of a person's heart, that evil thoughts come — sexual immorality, theft, murder, adultery, greed, malice, deceit, lewdness, envy, slander, arrogance and folly. All these evils come from inside and defile a person.*[111] Paul the Apostle wrote: *For by the grace given me I say to every one of you: Do not think of yourself more highly than you ought, but rather think of yourself with sober judgment, in accordance with the faith God has distributed to each of you.*[112] Evil thoughts, evil behavior and evil speech do not please God and have no place in the lives of those who fear him.

---

[111] Mark 7:21-23
[112] Romans 12:3

63

~The fear of the Lord adds length to life~

READ PROVERBS 10:27

Comment:

The idea of fear appears to be just one of many ways to distinguish between the good and the bad. Yet the thought of fear sets it apart as unique among the rest. Its explanation is beyond the normal. Fear toward God does contain the elements of awe and reverence, but in its simplest explanation is the realization that we are standing on holy ground which is the source of all good things. Yes, the good can die young and evil people may live long lives, but Proverbs 10:27, 9:11 as well as 3:16 give us another perspective on a life motivated by fear towards God. There is no doubt in my mind that God adds eternity to any life dedicated to him through Jesus Christ.

64

~*The fear of the Lord is a fountain of life*~

READ PROVERBS 14:2, 16, 26-27

Comment:

Anyone who fears God is on the right road, not deviating and wandering off in the wrong direction. Such a person keeps a level head and stays away from evil behavior. They maintain a safe environment for themselves and those in their care and protect them from harm. There's a saying that when we make plans, God laughs. It's good to make plans—just remember to have a Plan "B". Don't even count on a Plan "B" if you don't fear God: *The fear of the Lord is a fountain of life.* (verse 27) And: *The mouth of the righteous is a fountain of life.*[113] Also: *The teaching of the wise is a fountain of life.*[114] The thing they all have in common is a fountain filled with eternal life.

---

[113] Proverbs 10:11
[114] Proverbs 13:14

65

~Better a little with the fear of the Lord~

READ PROVERBS 15:16, 33

Comment:

A silent 1928 movie entitled "Our Dancing Daughters" starred Joan Crawford, Anita Page and Johnny "Mack" Brown (who later became a popular western movie star). At the conclusion of the movie, Anita Page is in a drunken stupor after an all night party. She brags about being married to the rich Johnny "Mack" Brown after taking him away from the "good" girl Joan Crawford, the real love of Brown. The movie ends when Page accidently falls down some stairs to her death and lands in front of three older women on their knees scrubbing the floor. One of the women picks up Page's hand adorned with several diamond bracelets which the camera zooms in on as the cleaning woman says, "Them won't do her no good now!"

66

~Through the fear of the Lord evil is avoided~

READ PROVERBS 16:6

Comment:

It is one's relationship with God through love and faithfulness that ignites the flames of fear toward God. Sin must be atoned for and avoided and this ultimately begins and ends with God and not through ceremony. It involves repentance and renewal but it has its roots in grace and forgiveness. One of my favorite hymns is "The Love of God" with words and music by Frederick M. Lehman, 1868-1953. The third stanza with chorus is:

Could we with ink the ocean fill and were
the skies of parchment made,
Were ev'ry stalk on earth a quill and ev'ry man a scribe by trade
To write the love of God above would drain the ocean dry,
Nor could the scroll contain the whole
tho stretched from sky to sky.

Chorus: O love of God, how rich and pure!
How measureless and strong!
It shall forevermore endure—the saints' and angels' song.[115]

---

[115] *Amazing Grace, 366 Inspiring Hymn Stories for Daily Devotions* by Kenneth W. Osbeck (Grand Rapids, MI: Kregel Publications, 1990), page 47.

67

~The fear of the Lord leads to life~

READ PROVERBS 19:23

Comment:

Fear toward God means we take God seriously and commit our lives to his care. This leads us to life eternal and being under God's care is enough to get us through all our trials and tribulations. Untouched by trouble means, in my opinion, that trouble won't trouble us! My son John and his wife Andrea operate Happy Wife Acres, a farm in Ohio where they care for chickens, rabbits, ducks, and bees. When I visit with them, I mingle with the chickens, the rabbits and the ducks, but I don't care to be around the bees, afraid of being stung! John and Andrea are also afraid of being stung and know the bees are capable and liable to attack them at any moment. But they know their bees and apparently their bees know them because everyone gets along with each other quite well!

68

~Humility is the fear of the Lord~

READ PROVERBS 22:4

Comment:

In the latest update of the New International Version, this verse is changed from *Humility and the fear of the Lord bring wealth and honor and life* to *Humility is the fear of the LORD; its wages are riches and honor and life*. The *and* between the word humility and the word fear (also seen in the King James Version) is an added word not in the original Hebrew. Humility and fear of the Lord go hand in hand. One complements the other. They are the basis for a religious life which puts God in control bringing all that is needed to make life worth living. It would solve a lot of problems to just say that humility is fear of the Lord. If it's possible to think in those terms, then this translation might be called the definitive Biblical reference to understanding Godly fear. I suppose any type of fear will humble a person. For instance, you don't see the losing side of a sports game shouting for joy over a possible loss. That's what makes understanding fear of the Lord so difficult. Rather, I should say that's what makes understanding fear of the Lord so different. We fear the Lord knowing we are never going to defeat him. In fact, our goal is not to defeat him. If eleven people were playing football against God alone, God could quit playing after the game started and the opposing team would still not be able to score! Just our association with the Lord is what enhances our lives and makes us winners! And that alone takes a lot of humility!

69

~Be zealous for the fear of the Lord~

READ PROVERBS 23:17-18

Comment:

John writes: *Dear friend, do not imitate what is evil but what is good. Anyone who does what is good is from God. Anyone who does what is evil has not seen God.*[116] Paul the Apostle encouraged others to imitate him.[117] Nothing wrong with that! Let your own life be a good example for others to follow. My son is 58 years old and operates a farm in Ohio after a career in the Air Force as a mechanical engineer with a degree from Auburn University, and a Masters in Business Administration and jobs with major business companies. He once told me how a fellow student in High School tried to interest him in drugs, but he turned him down with the comment that he did not want to involve himself in that manner of life!

---

[116] 3 John: 11
[117] 1 Corinthians 4:16-17

70

~Fear the Lord and do not join with the rebellious~

READ PROVERBS 24:21-22

Comment:

In his commentary on this verse, John Gill writes: "First the Lord, then the king; and such as fear the Lord are generally loyal to their king; the fear of God includes love to him, reverence of him, faith in him, submission to him, and the whole worship of him, inward and outward, attended with holiness of life and conversation…."[118] I think Gill is correct. Put the Lord first. Make sure you are on his bandwagon. That is, get on his agenda and everything else will fall into place. When you become a Christian, you don't start at the bottom and work your way up. You start at the top and with all executive privileges!

---

[118] *An Exposition of The Old Testament* by John Gill (Ireland: Industrial Printing School, 1853), Vol. 3, pages 561-562.

71

~Blessed is the one who always trembles before God~

READ PROVERBS 28:14

Comment:

I've included this verse which reads *trembles* because the New International Version in its newest update has changed the reading from *fears* to *trembles*. The King James Version has *feareth*. The Jewish Study Bible translates *is anxious* with the following note: "Here, *is anxious* (lit. 'fears') means fearing one's own sins and being willing to repent of them." The alternative, as stated in the rest of the verse, is to harden one's heart and fall into trouble. Deuteronomy 9:24 is a sad reminder from Moses regarding the Israelites: *You have been rebellious against the LORD ever since I have known you.* So, the idea of trembling before God can still help us understand that fearing God means being on his side.

72

~A woman who fears the Lord is to be praised~

READ PROVERBS 31:30

Comment:

My wife Catherine was a wonderful example of God's many graces bestowed upon someone who always put him in first place in her life. She always spoke of being "friends with God". But she never regarded God as owing her anything. She always recognized his superior status as Creator, Redeemer and Sustainer of life, especially her life. She saw life as a gift to be respected and enjoyed. After her death from brain cancer in 2018, I made a list of all her many interests and hobbies and put together a "Tribute to Cathy" which is available free in PDF format from the following Internet Link:

https://db.tt/6HnNdH6xwF

The Tribute is better appreciated watching from a computer—many pictures to view! I think Cathy feared the awesome power of God and therefore submitted herself completely to his Lordship, his rule, dominion and care. She wrote in the margin of her Bible: "Is the focus of my prayers on need, fear, weakness, or failure?"

These were all things she was obviously thinking about from her reading the story of King Jehoshaphat from 2 Chronicles, Chapter 20. She also wrote in the margin regarding what God had told the King to do regarding the King's problem: "God gave the solution—do nothing, v. 17." I read Verse 17 which said: *You will not have to fight this battle. Take up your positions; stand firm and see the deliverance the LORD will give you, O Judah and Jerusalem. Do not be afraid; do not be discouraged. Go out to face them tomorrow, and the LORD will be with you.* She faced every day of her life that way. And even on her last day on earth, she found victory in God!

73

~Whoever fears God will avoid all extremes~

READ ECCLESIASTES 7:15-18

Comment:

The writer of Ecclesiastes was a wise teacher. He reminds us that there is no one who never sins.[119] So, here in these verses he says it is best to live a moderate life: Don't overdo the good or the bad! Do not take either one to the extreme. It is wise to know we are not immune from sin; just guard against it. While the meaning of avoiding all extremes is unclear, it is, in my opinion, not justification for committing sin. Read also verses 13-14 in this same chapter. There are good times and there are bad times. Be happy in the good times and reflect in the bad times! I asked a gentleman once how he remained so trim. He said he learned when to push away from the table. Learn to push away from sin!

---

[119] Ecclesiastes 7:20

74

~It will go better with those who fear God~

READ ECCLESIASTES 8:12-13

Comment:

People who fear God are reverent toward God. They are reverent because they fear God. But just because you are reverent to God does not always mean you fear him. In other words, those who do not fear God can still be found to say nice things about God. It's hard to judge between the wicked and the righteous by how long they live and their success in life, but those who fear God will enjoy the blessings of eternity. The light of God will produce for them a lengthening shadow.

75

~*Fear God and keep his commandments*~

READ ECCLESIASTES 12:13-14

Comment:

Fearing God produces obedience to God. Just knowing that God is the judge of our every deed (openly or hidden, good or evil) is, in my opinion, enough evidence to fear him (and revere him, and worship him, and obey him). We cannot hide anything from God. I spell my name "Jimmie" not "Jimmy". It's on my birth certificate. I was in a particular government office on one occasion and was asked if I had ever spelled my name "Jimmy" to which I quickly responded "No". The person at the desk quickly showed me a document where in years past I had indeed signed my name "Jimmy". It was a mistake on my part which I had long forgotten. Fortunately the incident did nothing to prevent my transaction, but it was a lesson I shall not soon forget.

76

~The Lord Almighty is the one you are to fear~

READ ISAIAH 8:13

Comment:

I'm sure you have often felt bad about yourself and your personal situation and then learned about the misery endured by others due to sickness, bad weather, accidents, terrorists and the like. It doesn't lessen the pain of our own problems, but prayers in any of these dire situations prevail. There is only one true God, the Lord Almighty. If we can regard him as holy and fear him (and even tremble before him), we will conquer and prevail in life. As a child, we all have felt the comfort of holding on to our parents (or some significant person), and knowing we were in good hands. There are no stronger, loving, safer hands than those of the Lord Almighty.

77

~He will delight in the fear of the Lord~

READ ISAIAH 11:1-3

Comment:

In this Messianic passage the fear of the Lord is in very good company along with the Spirit of the Lord who grants (1) wisdom; (2) understanding; (3) counsel; (4) might; (5) knowledge; and (6) delight. When labeling this passage Messianic (which means "Anointed") it becomes prophetic. When the Hebrew "Messiah" is translated into Greek it becomes "Christ" the Son of God, fulfilled in Jesus. What a delight! Simon Peter made the declaration that Jesus was the Messiah to which Jesus replied that it was Jesus' Father in heaven who had revealed to Peter what to say. In other words, God confirmed that Jesus was the Messiah.[120]

---

[120] See Matthew 16:13-26

78

~The fear of the Lord is the key to this treasure~

READ ISAIAH 33:5-6

Comment:

Fearing the Lord is seen in this passage which shines in the midst of hard times and uniquely reveals the power of God which opens God's treasure house filled with justice, righteousness, salvation, wisdom and knowledge. Jesus told a parable about a merchant who was looking for pearls. When he found what he wanted, it would cost him lots of money. So he left and sold everything he had and bought it. The parable was about the kingdom of heaven, not about buying it but about being a part of it.[121] Jesus later told a man: *If you want to be perfect, go, sell your possessions and give to the poor, and you will have treasure in heaven. Then come, follow me.*[122]

---

[121] Matthew 13:45
[122] Matthew 19:21

79

~Why do you not fear me? ~

READ ISAIAH 57:11

Comment:

To put this in direct application to us today, God wants to know why we have so dreaded and feared other things to the point of following in their way of life as opposed to remembering God and thinking about him and his way of life. And then he reasons that maybe it's because he has not made himself known to us in a way that would cause us to fear and follow him. One needs to continue reading the rest of the passage where God says that when we eventually do call out for his help, obviously in desperation and not with any sincere change of heart, he will remind us to let our collection of idols save us! There are always people who will not heed the mandatory evacuation orders during a hurricane warning. God has his own orders for us to flee from sin.

80

*~Should you not fear me and
tremble in my presence?~*

READ JEREMIAH 5:22-25

Comment:

Scientific studies have shown that animals in the wild display fear when a predator is near. When this happens, the animals roam more often and eat less. When there are no predators there is no fear; animals multiply and the grasslands are devastated. I certainly don't see God as a predator, but the point is that when we have no fear of God, we live according to our own dictates of heart. Mere adoration does not always cause trembling: *The lion has roared and who will not fear? The Sovereign LORD has spoken — who can but prophesy?*[123]

---

[123] Amos 3:8

81

~I will inspire them to fear me~

READ JEREMIAH 32:38-41

Comment:

Is it possible to be inspired by God to fear him? God rejoices in doing good things for his children. To know that the Lord God loves me and wants me forever in his presence is enough to make me never want to turn away from him. God doesn't just wait around for us to discover his existence and concern for us. His Spirit is at work among those who fear him and miracles in the midst of misery do occur. Proclamations of God's majesty are being made worldwide every day. Good works in his Name are being accomplished among those in need. The Christian Church is not without its critics but it continues to grow and flourish in good deeds by good people. Even the evening news has moments of inspiration. Hopefully, eyes will see and ears will hear.

82

~To fear your name is wisdom~

READ MICAH 6:8-9

Comment:

Act justly, love mercy and walk humbly with God. These are acts requiring wisdom. And to fear God's Name—that is, to fear God Himself—imparts wisdom. The King James Version reads "see" instead of "fear". According to the Expositor's Bible Commentary[124] these words can be vocalized in Hebrew to read either way. See Psalm 86:11 where, in the King James Version, "fear" is used. There is a sound of alarm in this passage. Disaster (rod) is on its way and God is the One who appointed it. Fear God and be wise. Be wise and fear God.

---

[124] *The Expositor's Bible Commentary* (Digital by Zondervan Publishers).

83

~Surely you will fear me and accept correction!~

READ ZEPHANIAH 3:7

Comment:

The Bible describes God as patient, waiting for everyone to repent and not perish: *The LORD…is patient with you, not wanting anyone to perish, but everyone to come to repentance.*[125] We are also told that Jesus is God's gift to conquer death and enjoy eternal life: *For the wages of sin is death, but the gift of God is eternal life in Christ Jesus our LORD.*[126] God wants us to fear him and accept his correction. But we must not pretend to repent and then be eager to continue in our sins. God marvels that in spite of his warnings and discipline, the people are "eager" to continue their corrupt way of life.

---

[125] 2 Peter 3:9
[126] Romans 6:23

84

~I will come to put you on trial~

READ MALACHI 3:5-7

Comment:

To fear God is to turn away from any activity that displeases God. These include sorcerers, adulterers, perjurers, defrauding laborers of their wages, oppressing widows and orphans, and depriving aliens of justice. People who are guilty of doing these things (and many other bad things mentioned in the Bible) are people who do not fear God. This passage talks about God testifying against those who are being tried for turning away from his call to repentance. With God doing the testifying against you, what defense will you bring to your case? But there is hope found in verse 7: *Return to me, and I will return to you, says the LORD Almighty.*

85

~*A scroll of remembrance was written*~

READ MALACHI 3:16

Comment:

Those who fear the Lord and honor his name share something very special with one another. They are God's friends and their names are written in a scroll of remembrance. The Book of Revelation mentions a special book: *Anyone whose name was not found written in the book of life was thrown into the lake of fire.*[127] Now that I have a smart phone and discontinued my house phone, my name is no longer listed in the phone directory. Also, there are several people in the world who have the same name as mine. In God's Book, I'm sure he'll have it all worked out. Yes, I expect my name to be there and spelled correctly! If other names are identical, maybe mine will have my social security number beside it!

---

[127] Revelation 20:15

86

~His mercy extends to those who fear him~

READ LUKE 1:45-50, 74-75

Comment:

Mary believed that what the Lord God had said to her would be accomplished, proclaiming that God's mercy...*extends to those who fear him.* After the birth of John the Baptist, Zechariah's prophesy included the statement that God would ...*enable us to serve him without fear in holiness and righteousness before him all our days.* Our fear of God will keep us from being afraid when we serve him![128] As Christians, we believe in the all-sufficiency of Jesus Christ, our Lord and Savior of whom God said: *This is my Son, whom I love; with him I am well pleased.*[129]

---

[128] Exodus 20:20
[129] Matthew 3:17

87

~Don't you fear God?~

READ LUKE 23:39-43

Comment:

One of the two criminals being crucified along with Jesus made a request to Jesus which sounded very relevant, asking Jesus if he was the Messiah, to get them down from there! The second criminal's request was more realistic. He first rebuked his fellow criminal with: *Don't you fear God…since you are under the same sentence?* and reminded him that they deserved their punishment but that Jesus had done nothing wrong. Also, he had apparently seen the sign above Jesus which read "This is the King of the Jews" which led him to say: *Jesus, remember me when you come into your kingdom.* Then Jesus replied: *Truly I tell you, today you will be with me in paradise.*

88

~Living in the fear of the Lord~

READ ACTS 9:31

Comment:

This is quiet a statement concerning the early days of the Church: that all the Christians were enjoying a time of peace, growing in numbers and living in the fear of the Lord. But notice I left out a key ingredient—they were encouraged by the Holy Spirit! When the Holy Spirit is involved, it is God who is in control. I have fond memories of Early and Nancy Strickland who were members of Lee's Chapel Baptist Church in Middlesex, North Carolina, a church I served for 3 years while attending Southeastern Baptist Theological Seminary from 1965-68. It was a country church which was established in 1835 and is still going strong! Early was a retired farmer and a veteran of World War I. He would often get up "early" in the morning, sit in his rocking chair on the back porch of his home and appeared at times to be worrying. It was all in joking because Early was the community missionary, always driving his car around to check on the sick and shut-ins and delivering free produce from his garden which he and Nancy took care of. I told him, also in joking, that he should do all his worrying on one day and get it all over with for the week! Fearing God is something like my association with Early. It's as if God is saying: "Fear me and don't fear about anything else. Just cast all your fears on me and I'll take care of any other fears you may have." It reminds me of what the Apostle Peter wrote: *Humble yourselves, therefore, under God's mighty hand, that he may lift you up in due time. Cast all your anxiety on him because he cares for you.*[130]

---

[130] 1 Peter 5:6-7

89

~God accepts the one who fears him~

READ ACTS 10:34-35

Comment:

Fearing God opens the door to God's presence. In the Book of Esther, Mordecai wanted Queen Esther to make a request to the King. But if she approached the King without being summoned, she would be killed unless the King extended his gold scepter. Queen Esther did approach the King without being asked and the King was pleased to see her and held out the gold scepter.[131] She knew the rules and feared what might happen if her presence was not acceptable to the King. God accepts us into his presence. Jesus said: *Ask and it will be given to you; seek and you will find; knock and the door will be opened to you.*[132]

---

[131] Esther 4:9-11; 5:1-3
[132] Matthew 7:7

90

~Fear the Lord and persuade others~

READ 2 CORINTHIANS 5:11

Comment:

I can only assume that Paul, who says we know what it means to fear the Lord, that he is referring to the previous verse where he anticipates appearing before Christ for judgment. I'm not saying that won't happen, but why not get at least some of the judgment out of the way while we are here on earth? We need to take a good look at what we have done, are doing and planning to do—and get busy acknowledging our sins through confession. Indeed, Paul says in verse 17: *Therefore, if anyone is in Christ, the new creation has come: the old has gone, the new is here!* Making disciples should, in my opinion, bring about joy and celebration as we share with others our desire to please the Lord.

91

~Live as strangers in reverent fear~

READ 1 PETER 1:17

Comment:

We are not to live our lives in a fearful manner but in reverent fear toward God. Someone said that when they lost their sight, their biggest fear was losing their independence. Blind individuals and others with any kind of physical handicap work hard and successfully at maintaining their independence. My mother never wanted to live in a nursing home and died at age 89 without having to do so. Now as I have turned 82, I too cherish my independence. The fear that really matters is the reverent fear we have toward God, regardless of age. Reverent fear toward God will carry us safely to and through eternity which Jesus spoke about when he said he would return and take us to be with him in heaven.[133]

---

[133] John 14:3

92

~Fear God, give him glory and prepare for judgment~

READ REVELATION 14:6-7

Comment:

Everyone is invited to partake of the eternal gospel of God. We are called to fear God, give him glory, face his judgment, and worship him. Christians believe that God sent Jesus to die on the Cross to atone for our sins and resurrected him in preparation for our eternal life which begins the moment we accept Jesus as our Lord and Savior and receive the power of God's Holy Spirit. Fear toward God is a natural reaction to knowing that God loves me and his Spirit controls my life. God wants the very best for me and wants me to give my very best for him with his help. I want everything that goes with knowing God and I want at all times to please him as a loving child. Why then do I have to fear him? Well, because sometimes he might ask me to walk on water!

93

~Who will not fear you, O Lord,
and bring you glory?~

READ REVELATION 15:1-4

Comment:

While in Seminary, I wanted to write a book on Revelation from a historical perspective rather than prophesy. It would be over 35 years later before I did so. Against the downfall of the Roman Empire would be the people of God whose faith in Jesus Christ would secure their victory: *...over the beast and its image and over the number of its name.* Christians rejoice in triumph singing a new song of deliverance as Moses rejoiced at the Red Sea. Their new song reflects their victory and joy of salvation in Jesus Christ. To fear God and sing the song of Moses and the song of the Lamb is an eternal privilege and honor.[134]

---

[134] For the song of Moses and the song of the Lamb see Exodus 15:1 and Revelation 5:9-10; 14:3.

94

~Praise our God, all who fear him~

READ REVELATION 19:5-9

Comment:

God's servants are the ones who fear him, praise him, love him, and honor him. Fear that is filled with praise, love and honor is a powerful reaction deserving of God! "Hallelujah" means "Praise God" and we are called upon to: *...rejoice and be glad and give him glory! For the wedding of the Lamb has come, and his bride has made herself ready.* Our union with Christ is made possible because of our faith in him who in turn bestows upon us his own righteousness and prepares us to attend *...the wedding supper of the Lamb!*

A SUMMARY STATEMENT

In my book "Bad Things from the Good Book" I listed events in the Bible that I thought were bad for someone. All sin is bad in the eyes of God. God is holy and does not tolerate sin. But what is sin? From God's standpoint it is anything he does not like. In order to find out what that is, one must go through the Bible and find out what pleases God and what doesn't please him. He gave us the Ten Commandments, so that's a good place to start. And then there are places in the Bible where God declares his hate for certain actions, such as mistreating widows and orphans. Then there are direct statements throughout the Bible about what is good, such as honest weights. In the Old Testament there were many things that should be done in a certain way that, at least in the minds of most Christians, are no longer required, such as eating certain foods or offering sacrifices on an altar.

What I found when researching for bad things in the Bible was that I discovered God was guilty of doing some things which he did not want others to do. One of the Ten Commandments is not to commit murder. Yet God, on many occasions in the Bible, takes the lives of people. In the Genesis account of the flood, God destroys the lives of everyone on earth except Noah and his family. The only answer I have for that is there must be some dynamic between a holy God and sinful people that is the same as earthly people defending themselves against an adversary. Whatever it is, as we would say in the military where I spent almost thirty years, the answer is beyond my pay grade. In my previous book about bad things in the Bible, I included the verses that have God taking drastic action against those who disobeyed him. God expected his people to fear him and be faithful to him as a result of his signs and wonders and his discipline. In this present book I have centered my attention on verses that call us to fear God in a way that pleases him; and his promise in return is always that our lives will be filled with his blessings.

I am a Christian and have been for seventy years. I'm a retired minister and military chaplain with lots of religious training and experience, but I don't claim to know everything about the Bible. But I have no doubt in my own mind that my loyalty, as I live and when I die, is with God, his Spirit, and his Son Jesus the Messiah, a loyalty that is secured for eternity. And I believe that in that eternity, any unanswered questions I have about God and the Bible will be answered to my satisfaction.

So, why have I written this book about fearing God? I alluded to this at the beginning of the book, but to be more specific, I had another concern (about fearing God) that I've been unable to fully understand. Books have been written and sermons are popular on the subject of how to overcome fear in life. Throughout the Bible we are told to have faith and not to fear; that God will be with us to comfort and guide us. And then, I began to see all these verses about how the really righteous people are those who fear God. Furthermore, we are told that God wants us to fear him. Most of the answers I kept getting from those who were dealing with this issue were that fearing God was just a phrase which really meant to adore, give reverence to, and worship God. And I discovered that such an answer was partly true. But I felt there had to be more to it than that. One source which I did not discover until finishing this book was Dr. David Jeremiah's book *What Are You Afraid Of?:*

Facing down Your Fears with Faith. The last chapter in his book deals with fearing God. Dr. Jeremiah definitely gives the reader a clear understanding that fearing God means exactly what the Bible proclaims. When I found so many references in the Bible about fearing God, I wanted to know why were they translated fear instead of revere? As I have tried to explain elsewhere in this book, there must be a relationship between our fear of God and his greatness, his glory, his omnipotence (all-powerful), omniscience (all-knowing), and omnipresence (everywhere at the same time). It's when we don't fear him that we begin to ignore him and disregard him. So, with this view, when we fear God we can better control our earthly fears.

Now, what I have done is gathered from these many verses about fearing God what I consider is pertinent to understanding what is meant by fearing God. Here is my list, not in any particular order of importance. Some items are similar and I'm sure I've overlooked others. Please make your own list. The idea is to better understand what is involved in fearing God. I find it really complex! As a matter of fact, it seems to me that when someone finds out about something, there is always a difference of opinion found somewhere else. But I already knew that, having been a marriage counselor for many years!

Here's my list gained directly from the Bible verses presented in this book to better understand what fearing God means:

> Hate dishonest gain
> Enjoy protection from sin
> Be helpful to the disabled
> Be forgiving
> Be against injustice, partiality, bribery
> Be devoted to your friends
> Shun all evil, despise vile things
> Speak the truth

- Be a good example to others
- Follow only the one true God
  - Acknowledge God's power
  - Have reverence for God
  - Give Him your most precious gift
  - Obey Him, walk in His ways
  - Be good and desire His will
  - Make Him your stronghold
  - Keep His commandments
  - Love Him, serve Him, praise Him
  - Recognize His wonderful gifts
  - Take refuge in Him
  - Live with hope in His love
  - Revel (delight) in His righteousness
  - Treasure His words
  - Rejoice in the Lord
  - Trust in His Holy Name
  - Fulfill your vows to Him
  - Receive His salvation
  - Tell what God has done for you
  - Proclaim His love
  - Trust in His care
  - Enjoy His presence in your life
  - Accept and enjoy His blessings
  - Listen and learn from Him
    - Gain wisdom and knowledge
    - Seek His teachings and guidance

What fear of the Lord actually is and does:

- Keeps us from sinning
- Imparts Wisdom

- Pure, enduring forever
- Causes hatred of evil
- Source of life, salvation, wealth, honor
- Brings blessings and praise
- Extends mercy
- Brings glory to God

As I've mentioned before, my concern is primarily with the importance of fearing God, in spite of the fact that the Bible has a lot to say about trusting God and not being afraid of life. I do hope that you can at least appreciate my efforts and maybe have gained some incite of how fear of God is associated with his majesty and power, an association and intimacy which is capable of improving our lives in relationship to God and one another. We should in some way, in speaking or writing about God or just living a Godly life, communicate that we have full respect and adoration toward God as our Spiritual Power; that we feel fully accountable to Him in everything we do; and then maintain a lifestyle that clearly reflects our faith, hope and love in Him and which demonstrates clearly that we fear His displeasure any time and in any way we fail to acknowledge Jesus as Lord and Savior. Personally, I believe that if we cannot determine and make known that anyone (including ourselves) who participates in evil things are people who do not fear God, then we need to re-evaluate our own fear and relationship with the Almighty.

Jimmie Leon Hancock, February, 2020

REFERENCES CONSULTED

BIBLES

Contemporary English Version, The Promise™ Study Edition (Nashville: Thomas Nelson Publishers, 1996).

Complete Jewish Bible, Translation by David H. Stern (Clarksville, MD: Messianic Jewish Publishers, 1998).

Jewish Study Bible, Edited by Adele Beerlin and Marc Zvi Brettler (New York: Oxford University Press, 2004).

The Holy Bible, New International Version®, NIV® Biblica, Inc.™ (Grand Rapids, MI: Zondervan, 2011).

The Holy Bible, Authorized King James Version (Nashville: Holman Bible Publishers, 1982).

New American Bible, The Catholic Study Bible (Oxford, New York: Oxford University Press, 1990).

ELECTRONIC SOFTWARE

Biblesoft PC Study Bible, Version 5 (Seattle, WA, Biblesoft, Inc., 2003).

Logos Bible Software, Version 8 (Faithlife Corporation, 2000-2020)

Encyclopedia of Jewish Women on the web.

OTHER RESOURCES

Adeney, Walter F., *The Expositor's Bible: Ezra, Nehemiah and Esther* (London: Hodder and Stoughton Publishers, Second Edition, 1906).

Baker, Kenneth L. & John R. Kohlenberger III, *Zondervan NIV Bible Commentary, Vol. I: Old Testament, An Abridgment of the Expositor's Bible Commentary* (Grand Rapids: Zondervan Publishing House, 1994).

Bratcher, Robert G. & William D. Reyburn, *A Handbook on Psalms* (New York: United Bible Societies, 1991).

Bruce, F. F., General Editor, *New International Bible Commentary* (Grand Rapids, MI: Zondervan, 1979).

Butler, Trent C., General Editor, *Holman Bible Dictionary* (Nashville: Holman Bible Publishers, 1991).

Gaebelein, Frank E., General Editor, *The Expositor's Bible Commentary,* 12 Volumes on Interactive Disc, Version 2.5.1 (Grand Rapids, MI: Zondervan Publishing House).

Gill, John, *An Exposition of the Old Testament*, Volume 3 (Ireland: Industrial Printing School, 1853).

Hancock, Jimmie L., *Bad News from the Good Book, With 98 Engravings by Austave Doré* (Lulu Publishing Services, 2010).

Hancock, Jimmie L., *Tribute to Cathy* (Unpublished, 2019).

Jeremiah, David, *What Are You Afraid Of?* (Carol Stream, Illinois: Tyndale House Publishers, Inc., 2013).

Lewis, C. S., *The Joyful Christian* (New York: Macmillan Publishing Co., Inc., 1977).

McLain, Bill, *Do Fish Drink Water?* (New York: MJF Books, 1999).

Osbeck, Kenneth W., *Amazing Grace—365 Inspiring Hymn Stories for Daily Devotions* (Grand Rapids, MI: Kregel Publications, 1990).

Wigoder, Geoffrey, General Editor, *The Illustrated Dictionary & Concordance of the Bible* (New York: Sterling Publishing, 2005).

Printed in the United States
By Bookmasters